# BUILDING RESILIENCE

The 7 Steps to Creating **Highly Successful** Lives

## LES DUGGAN AND MARK SOLOMONS

Published by Developing Potential Group 2014

A CIP Catalogue record for this book is available from the British Library.

The moral rights of the author have been asserted.

Illustrations provided by Pyrink.

Design and formatting by ebook-designs.co.uk

ISBN - 978-0-9931006-0-4

# ACKNOWLEDGEMENTS

To everyone we have worked with, supported and learnt from – thank you. You have provided the inspiration for us to choose the path we now pursue, supporting the next generation in giving them the best chance for successful lives.

This book has been written for the teaching profession. Both of us have teachers in our immediate family and a long-standing interest in education.

You all inspire us; the students, teachers, support staff and school leaders we meet. We would like to particularly thank all those from schools who were involved in helping us write this book and who provided us with feedback and gave reviews of the first draft manuscript. They are listed below (in alphabetical order by surname) and thank you to each and every one of you. Your support is very much needed and appreciated.

Chris Barns, Assistant Head
Attleborough High School

Helen Blachford, Curriculum Leader PSCHE
Priory School, Southsea

Richard Brown, Headteacher
The Urswick School, Hackney, London

Ian Colling, Headteacher
Magdalen College School, Brackley

Pauline Crothers, Head of Third Year
Kingston Grammar School

Chris Evans, Head of Key Stage 4
Heckmondwike Grammar School

Eddie Falshaw, Deputy Head
Leighton Park School, Reading

Claire George, Assistant Head
Clitheroe Royal Grammar School

Kathryn Hardy, Deputy Head
Allestree Woodlands School, Derby

Phil Jones, Associate Headteacher
Head of The Stanway Federation Learning Centre

Linda Lindan, Head of Wellbeing
MERIT Medical PRU, Stoke-on-Trent

Liz McIntosh, Headteacher
Tunbury Primary School, Chatham

Linda McQuone, Deputy Head
Blackminster School, Evesham

Karen Muir, Headteacher
Ladywell School, Glasgow

Laura O'Shaughnessy, Assistant Head
Partnership Development Manager, Essex

Derek Peaple, Headteacher
Park House School, Newbury

Ursie Phayre, Mentor Teacher and Teacher Coach
Kenya and Tanzania

Lissa Samuels, Headteacher
Cayley School, Tower Hamlets, London

Bob Simpson, Deputy Headmaster
Merchant Taylors' Boys, Crosby

Michaela Still, Assistant Principal/Consultant Leader
Ossett Academy

Nikki Wall, Counsellor
St. Peters Catholic Voluntary Academy, Middlesborough

Ted Walker, Regional Director
Academies Improvement, Erudition Schools Trust

Simon White, Head of School
Wellsway School, Bristol

David Woodhouse, Co-ordinator
Liverpool Learning Trust

# CONTENTS

# FOREWORD

When my husband Andrew got off the boat, just two weeks into our 3000 mile two-man Atlantic Rowing Challenge, it turned out to be the best thing that ever happened to me.

It forced me to deal with changes that I didn't expect to face and would never have chosen. Should I get on the rescue boat or carry on alone? I was faced with a choice between the security of the rescue boat and automatic disqualification from the race, or going on alone. Three other crews had previously gone solo – all of them far more experienced oarsmen than me – and none of them had made it. They were all big and experienced rowers, while I was a novice who hadn't rowed before.

As I watched the rescue boat sail away, I knew they didn't believe that I could do this, but what mattered was that I believed I could.

I had to come up with strategies and techniques to pick myself up and carry on and this book is a practical guide that will help you build resilience and pursue those things you want in life.

I was 26 years old when I crossed the Atlantic and learnt so much about what I could achieve, and to be able to share these attitudes and skills with young people at school is something that will set them up for their successful lives.

The strategies and techniques shared in the book are ones common to successful people. When I was on the boat I learnt how to play 'movies' in my mind to overcome fear – by mentally rehearsing again and again all of the possible outcomes of a situation, the fear of the unknown was dramatically reduced – it had become almost 'known' and set out just what I wanted to happen. I learnt how to ask for help and saw the importance of having a support team around me. I also developed a passionate belief that I would make it, even when others doubted me.

Most of all I learnt that, although we can't choose or control many of our circumstances, we can all choose our attitude, every day.

This book sets out how you can do this for yourself and your students. It provides explanations, exercises, and stories and takes you through seven steps you can use yourself and with your students, to develop their self-belief and give them the skills and positive approach to tackle everything that life will throw their way.

I started my career as a PE teacher, and since then have spent 10 years as a board member for The Duke of Edinburgh's Award. I am passionate about equipping our young people, not just with qualifications, but with resilience so that they can face life's challenges. If we can choose the right attitude, there is every possibility of achieving even the biggest goals.

**Debra Searle MVO, MBE. Professional Adventurer, Diversity Ambassador, author and television presenter (www. debrasearle.com).**

The publication of a book about resilience could not be more timely. The generation of young people in our schools today are, at one and the same time, both the most and least tested in our educational history. The most tested in that they have been subject to more target-driven and modular assessment than any other; the least in that a combination of technological and societal change has simultaneously reduced the opportunities for them to test themselves, their resolve and character.

Their ability to develop resilience, through no fault of their own, has been diminished. And yet at the same time this paradox of more testing and less testing poses its own challenge in terms of resilience. Young people find themselves under increasing pressure to succeed against the backdrop of a popular culture defined by summarily dispensed X-Factor-style judgements. Fame – or failure – is apparently instantaneous, and absolute. The process of learning, of building character through setback and success, challenge and support, is somehow missing. Andy Warhol's famous dictum has never been more appropriate.

For educators, Les and Mark's exploration and reflection on the development of resilience as a learning process, centrally positioned with our curriculum, is to be warmly welcomed. I have no doubt that it will contribute significantly to more and more of our young people responding positively to the challenges of 21st century life and realising their amazing potential.

**Derek Peaple, Headteacher, Park House School, Newbury**

# ENDORSEMENTS

This book provides a very useful and accessible practical guide for teachers and parents, to help them create a positive environment to support young people to build resilience and achieve success.

**Baroness Sue Campbell CBE**

There's nothing more important to a young person's learning than 'resilience'. Without it they will never be the people they could become. Teachers are always trying to find ways to help students build it. Here is an invaluable map and set of strategies that will help teachers, parents and youngsters themselves to do just that. I wish I had had it at my side both as a parent and a teacher.

**Sir Tim Brighouse**

We are a specialist support to inclusion, whose bread and butter is empowering learners to become emotionally literate, mindful self leaders. Your book reinforces all that is vital in this area, linking emotions to thoughts and actions and building happy, positive lives.

Your book is a very easy read for teachers and is for all learners. It reaches out to the most disengaged but also gives solution focused strategies for switched-on learners.

**Karen Muir, Headteacher,**
**PPR Inclusion Service, Ladywell School, Glasgow**

Your book does not really define resilience against the criteria that Moore and others use and in that sense, it is a fresh departure from the work of Bonnie Bernard and Werner and Smith that originated in North America. It also offers another perspective on Lyn Worsley's 'resilience doughnut.'

As a motivational tool I can take much from this and am keen to explore at least some of the steps here at Merchant Taylors', including looking at DISC profiling.

There is little doubt that at a time when the need to motivate students has never been greater, books such as this allow us to explore a range of approaches.

**Bob Simpson, Deputy Headmaster,
Merchant Taylors' Boys, Crosby**

This is a much needed resource! 'Building Resilience' will help busy teachers infuse their lessons (and whole school culture) with the essential skills and qualities every individual needs to have in place in order to learn and to deal with life. This book helps to provide the frequently overlooked, and largely absent, foundations of education without which exam success can be difficult and/or meaningless.

A little thought and a collective approach to putting these ideas into existing practice in a school, would transform the learning culture rapidly.

**Linda Lindan, Head of Wellbeing,
MERIT Medical PRU, Stoke-on-Trent**

I really enjoyed the book – I think the thing I enjoyed the most was the fact that it's packed full of stories and anecdotes but also suggested ways to use them with children and classes. I shall certainly be using a lot of these ideas in lessons, and particularly in assemblies.

**Linda McQuone, Deputy Head,
Blackminster School, Evesham**

In order for children to be successful in school and into adult life it has become increasingly clear that we need to help build resilience in our children and young people. The value of a well-constructed curriculum, which teaches students how to learn, how to deal with life's challenges and how to continue to grow despite setbacks, is an essential element of modern education. Les and Mark's book gives educators a range of clear ideas about how we can better provide for this essential component in the life of young people today.

**Simon White, Head of School,
Wellsway School, Bristol**

I thought the book was great. It serves as a great reminder of what a teacher can do to impact the lives of students beyond the teaching of subject material. The stories of recognised names that they can relate to is really useful to show that the information is real as opposed to yet another 'theory' made up by some old teacher type.

I am forever trying to incorporate more work on resilience through whole school PSHE and this book will allow me to direct staff to the evidence to support my claims. I see a rise in stress every year and you hit the nail on the head in the book as to why this is. Thankfully, the book now sets out a clear path towards helping reduce this trend.

**Chris Evans, Head of Key Stage 4,**
**Heckmondwike Grammar School, Heckmondwike**

'Building Resilience' should be a key document to accompany the reviewed national curriculum. It is an easy to read, practical guide for primary and secondary practitioners to use when planning lessons or assemblies for children as part of their SMSC education. The success stories provide tangible examples to illustrate the importance of resilience as a skill, which all children need to support their development and prepare them for life in modern Britain.

**Liz McIntosh, Headteacher,**
**Tunbury Primary School, Chatham, Kent**

I spent a rewarding evening reading your book. That in itself is a quality – a busy teacher will have time for this. It is a useful refresher for experienced teachers and I would recommend it to new members of the teaching profession. It could also be regarded as a self-help tool for Sixth Formers.

**Richard Brown, Headteacher,
The Urswick School, Hackney, London**

Your book is just so timely – it seems to be the hot topic for staff and parents – it's good that we acknowledge that resilience can be taught and also reassuring that their anxieties can be mostly lessened. Being able to signpost to the whole book or specific parts will be very useful – when is it going to print? I know many of my staff will be wanting to buy!

**Kathryn Hardy, Deputy Head,
Allestree Woodlands School, Derby**

I thoroughly enjoyed reading the book – it is written in such an engaging way with real examples in abundance – and with a wide range of practical ways for teachers to undertake what is such an important part of their role!

Thank you for sharing the book with me – it really was a pleasure to read it and I now have a number of ideas (in addition to using the Successful Lives programme) for how to build resilience within our young people.

**Helen Blachford, Curriculum Leader PSCHE,
Priory School, Southsea**

I love the introduction/foreword, as it explains the context very clearly and without jargon. Anyone could pick it up and understand easily. I thought that the seven steps were also explained very clearly and concisely, and were quite inspirational! I liked that the book is not too heavy on academic theory, which makes it an enjoyable read. I also liked the two simple steps for teachers about sharing and developing resilience with students, which is crucial.

**Michaela Still, Assistant Principal / Consultant Leader, Ossett Academy and Sixth Form College, Ossett**

I really enjoyed the book, it contains valuable advice for teachers, parents and young people, tempered with anecdotal and real-life stories which brings the theory to life. I particularly enjoyed the DISC and Grow sections and felt they were accessible and applicable to a range of situations, for both adults and young people.

The appendix guide to the seven steps is a useful reminder of the key points of the book; it is a quick reference guide, which is useful for refreshing the most important points.

**Nikki Wall, Counsellor, St. Peters Catholic Voluntary Academy, Middlesborough**

The book maintains the attention of the reader because it challenges and encourages reflection on current practice and provides the opportunity to think about how learning can be more effective for the young people involved in the process. The activities provided help the reader to explore the ideas in some depth and engage with the content.

The seven steps is a systematic approach to build resilience that can easily be followed as a guide by professionals working in education. Tutors would also benefit from the ideas in the book and it would stimulate thinking and planning to make tutoring more effective in supporting young people to make progress in their learning.

**Phil Jones, Associate Headteacher, Head of The Stanway Federation learning Centre, Stanway, Essex**

Really enjoyed reading this and it has come at a great moment in education when the well being, mental and physical, of pupils is a hot topic. Rightly so, given the new pressure faced by young people today, pressures that I for one never had to cope with.

Overall, I think this book would be a fantastic addition to schools that are genuinely making an effort to build resilience.

**Eddie Falshaw, Deputy Head,
Leighton Park School, Reading**

# INTRODUCTION

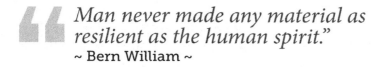

*Man never made any material as resilient as the human spirit."*
~ Bern William ~

Young people are the world's greatest asset. Every day presents an opportunity to acquire the tools, knowledge, and wisdom, which will help them grow into successful adults, and make their mark in the world. As a teacher or parent, you can support them to develop their strengths, talents, and character to enable them to overcome any of life's challenges. One of these traits is resilience or the ability to respond positively to setbacks and the good news is that it can be taught.

Through a combination of business and leadership experience, we have found effective and easy to implement solutions, for teachers and others who are dedicated to help children create a stronger and healthier mindset and make more of their unique talents. We have already shared these with well over a hundred thousand young people, through an educational charity we helped to establish.

Resilience is important in life because it can make the difference between success and failure, growing or stagnating, flourishing or floundering. It underpins achieving potential and making dreams a reality.

Why do so many of today's students lack resilience?

Most people agree that children are our most precious gift, and as a result, many parents like to coddle and protect them from life's difficulties. They want childhoods to be enchanted and delightful. While that is understandable, we have removed many of the challenges that give them the opportunity to grow and develop natural resilience.

Children are given far less credit than they deserve for being able to bounce back from their trials and tribulations. Remember when you were a child and the difficult experiences you had that helped you learn and grow. They may have been daunting at first, but through your effort, you gained strength, built character, and developed resilience.

We have become risk averse as a society. Many parents no longer let their children play outside because of fear for their safety. As we have become a more litigious society, schools have moved to ban some school trips or more challenging activities, and before anything can be acted upon, an often onerous risk assessment process has to be undertaken. While managing risks appropriately is important, we have perhaps let the pendulum swing too far and are stopping our young people from taking risks and learning from them.

In addition, we seem to spend so much of our time 'spoon-feeding' students to pass exams or watching them move through school on a conveyor belt, while we are too busy to provide the individual or character building attention that is often needed.

The Confederation of British Industry and many global employers are challenging the current school system, to produce more students who have better 'employability' skills – many of the softer skills, such as resilience, understanding values and behaviour and having the right attitude.

As we continue to focus largely on academic and exam performance, are we letting down many of our students, as well as contributing to poorer future economic competitiveness on the world stage. Even though we continue to push up exam result targets (for example, 5 GCSEs, including English and Maths), the results we accept still mean too many young people leave schools with poor skills.

We have to have a greater focus on preparing them for a successful life after school, enabling them to self-manage and overcome the many challenges they will face – particularly for those from more challenging backgrounds.

We realise that there is no, one size fits all solution and that the things we propose may not win favour with everyone or be right for every individual. We have written a guide full of practical suggestions that we know will make a difference for many young people (and adults too) and you can choose the ones that you think will work for you and your students.

What is contained in this book is the start of a conversation that teachers and adults can have with students. It is about building resilience and character, and it is equally as important for young people as reading, writing, and mathematics. It probably underpins the reason that you wanted to be an educator – you were driven by a passion to help young people, as well as a love of the subjects you teach.

Everything you will discover about building resilience in your students will enable you to support their growth and development and hopefully renew your excitement for what you do. It will engage them as they begin to understand that having resilience is one of the keys to having a successful life.

This is based on 20 years of experience working with and developing successful leaders in business, education and sport, and other elite performers, such as Olympians. We have spent much of this time helping people change the behaviours and habits that have often prevented them from achieving their goals.

In 2007, we set up our first educational charity and established a new purpose. We asked ourselves why we spent so much of our lives helping older people change, when we could help more young people develop the right habits in the first place, which they can use for the whole of their successful lives.

As a result, we recently launched *Successful Lives*, a set of lessons and resources to support school leaders and teachers develop the skills you will read about in this book. Academic achievement is very important and adding the qualities, skills, behaviours, and habits of successful people (character), will mean far more young people really do achieve their full potential.

We hope you will become part of this educational movement and if you want to find out more and receive regular tips then visit www.successfullives.co.uk/resilience. Your password is Build-it-Now. We look forward to seeing you there.

**Mark Solomons**

**Les Duggan**

# CHAPTER ONE: EMBRACING RESILIENCE

Our attitudes are important when it comes to being successful. This starts from a very early age. The toddler who is learning to walk will fall down many times before they master the skill. An athlete who wants to excel will practise for hours after everyone else has gone home, in an attempt to gain mastery of their sport. The student, who wishes to progress in life and perhaps attend a university, will study extensively to ensure good grades and entrance exam scores. None of these examples can take place without the right attitude, one that is resilient and determined.

Any worthwhile achievement in life is made through effort and commitment by overcoming challenges and driving for success. Resilience is an attitude of mind that enables us to bounce back and fulfil our dreams and aspirations.

*"Any worthwhile achievement in life is made through effort and commitment by overcoming challenges and driving for success."*

## Seven Steps (Ps) to Building Resilience

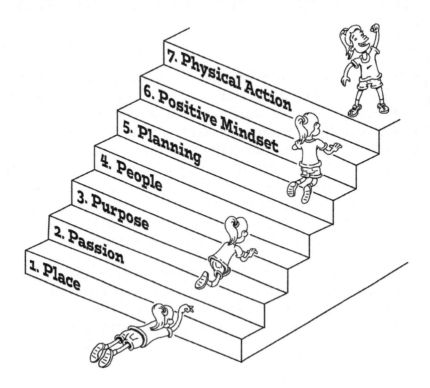

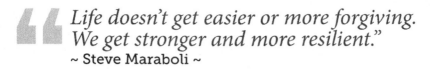

*Life doesn't get easier or more forgiving.*
*We get stronger and more resilient."*
~ Steve Maraboli ~

Life has many steps that help you grow and learn, sometimes making it seem as if you're climbing all 29,000 feet of Everest, the highest mountain in the world, without a break. Yet learning just seven steps to build resilience will enable any young person to develop the skills and attitudes needed, to climb what is in front of them each day.

The seven steps is a proven model that has helped young people and students, as well as many adults, learn the positive habit of resilience.

Each of the seven steps you learn will be covered in greater detail in future chapters. Below is a summary of each one, so you can begin to understand the whole process.

1) **Place**: People often put themselves in a place of comfort and security. This is understandable because they need to feel safe and secure. Yet to develop potential, you need to take risks and step outside your comfort zone. The places and situations you allow yourselves to explore are often limited by your own self-confidence. Yet opportunities for discovering who you truly are and what you are capable of, come from stretching yourself and attempting to try new things.

   Moving out of your comfort zone can be scary, but it is where you can achieve things that you once thought impossible. It's where the person, who was afraid to speak in front of others, delivers a fantastic presentation. It's where the individual afraid of roller coasters, finds out that they overcame their fear and actually enjoyed the experience.

2) **Passion**: Every child has innate curiosity and a desire to learn. It is passion that fuels progress and achievement. Great passion is associated with your heart and is the foundation of all of your motivation. Everyone has something that inspires them, something that intrigues them, even if they can't quite figure out why. Finding passion is essential to give young people the energy and drive to start new projects and ventures. When things go wrong, it will give them the resilience to bounce back and achieve their goals and dreams.

**3) Purpose**: People want to achieve goals and be successful, but what drives human beings is having meaning and purpose in what they do and meeting the challenges they take on. Part of your intrinsic motivation is to learn and develop, to experience what life offers and to play a role in being co-creators in the world. You make a difference by who you are, as well as what you do. An essential element of your purpose is to take your strengths and talents, and develop them, so that you can be personally successful and make a contribution to society.

To deliver on your life's purpose, note the thoughts of Michelangelo when he said:

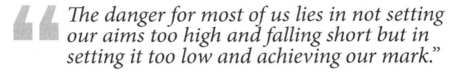

*The danger for most of us lies in not setting our aims too high and falling short but in setting it too low and achieving our mark."*

So understanding your purpose (also called a vision), where you harness your talents and be of service to others, will enable you to truly fulfil your potential and build the resilience and strength to overcome any obstacles that life puts in front of you.

**4. People**: Life will always be full of challenges and people can succeed on their own, but the support of caring people who understand dreams and goals, can make a big difference. Therefore, for any young person setting out in life, the opportunity to develop a network and group of supporters is really important.

The people that you allow to impact your life are closely connected to the planning step above. There may be some people who laugh at your dreams and it is important to realise that you can decide whether you let them affect your confidence or not. Learning whom to trust comes with experience and maturity, and making young people aware that they have choices as to what they accept from others, is a gift that you, as a positive role model, can give them.

It can make all the difference for young people, who may feel inferior or overawed, due to their parents not seeing their potential, or deciding to accept that their life is destined to be difficult and unrewarding. Attracting positive people, particularly adults, to be supporters can make a young person feel they are really valued and capable.

5. **Planning**: Having a purpose and vision is empowering but without goals and an action plan, they are but dreams. A vision needs to be something you aspire to and seemingly just beyond your reach, but goals need to be tangible, realistic, and time framed.

Planning is about you. It is about what you are willing to do, to achieve your goals in life. As part of the planning process, you will find that there are some things that you can influence and some things that you can't control.

Aspects of life may be outside your control, such as the authority of parents and teachers, life events, health, the people you meet; however, you will find that there are two areas where you have choice and influence. These are your own personal attitude and focus. It is also helpful when planning for success, to surround yourself with positive people who will support you in pursuing your dreams and who have the character traits you would like.

Planning helps you create a route map for your success. If you want to be a writer, you are going to look for inspiration and learn about how various authors became successful. If you love basketball and want to have a 90%

free-throw success rate, you may study a basketball great such as Michael Jordan and learn what he did to become one of the greatest in the game. Later in this book you will be introduced to the G.R.O.W. Model (Goal, Reality, Options, Will), which will help you plan your route one step at a time.

6. **Positive Mindset**: Mindset is an important factor in achieving success. It can be your greatest asset and also your biggest enemy and critic. Positive mindset springs from positive thoughts and manifests itself in a 'can do attitude', regardless of what happens. When you are positive, you always see life as a glass half full, rather than half empty.

According to Dr Barbara Fredrickson[1], a well-known American Psychologist, we need to have internal dialogue (self talk) in a ratio of at least 3:1 positive to negative, in order to build self-belief and create resilience. The most effective way to do this is to be mindful of your thoughts, let negative ones go and focus on the positive. Enabling young people to recognise that it is normal to have negative thoughts and to be able to manage them and focus on a positive 'can do' mantra; will build a winning mindset.

7. **Physical Action**: Physical action has two dimensions.

   i.     Building physical capability; and

   ii.    Taking action physically, to make things happen.

Being physically well and energised, underpins all performance and to achieve any dream you have to take action to move forward.

---

1 See the list of references on page 209 for more information on Dr Barbara Fredrickson and her positivity ratio.

While clarity of thought and a positive attitude are important, the physical body also plays a fundamental role in building resilience and character. Well-nourished and properly exercised bodies, give the energy to support people in their everyday challenges. Taking care of your body by treating it with respect, is an important habit to develop when young. It is the vehicle that will enable you to achieve what you want out of life. We're not talking about perfection, just maximising your physical capability though positive choices when it comes to eating, sleeping, and exercise.

As well as physical capability, this step includes embracing physical action by making positive choices and committing your time and energy to action. It is only by taking the first steps towards achieving your goals, that you will be able to fulfil your dreams.

The seven steps are a cohesive system that helps build resilience. Each one supports young people in developing strategies, which will enable them to be successful and overcome obstacles and setbacks.

## The Teacher's Role

Teachers have many demands on their time and every minute of the day is valuable and often planned out. However, there are two things you can do immediately to help your students build resilience.

Firstly, be great role models and secondly, share from your own experiences and the learning from this book, which comes from working with successful leaders, managers and coaches, many of whom have also developed successful adults and young people.

Resilience will:

- Help students take personal responsibility for their lives.
- Help them use their strengths and plan for success.
- Enable them to build effective networks of support.
- Help them to understand their unique place in the world.
- Build self-confidence and self-belief.
- Encourage them to be healthy and to take action.
- Be a gift you can share with students – one that will empower them on their life's journey.

As a teacher, you embrace resilience every day, overcoming obstacles, finding solutions to problems and keeping positive when facing challenges. You are adaptable, flexible, and most of the time you are confident that you can achieve things. The thought of sharing this quality with your students is hopefully exciting. Seeing how you can empower them in their lives, will reinforce your sense of purpose.

## Fast Start: Two Simple Steps

If you are not already doing them, there are two simple steps that you can take to make a fast start. They are:

1. **Work towards developing positive mindsets in your students**. Below are suggestions of how you might do this by asking students to share:

    i.    One thing they did well during a lesson that day.

ii.   Three things they did well during the full day.

iii.  One thing they were excited and enthused by during the day.

iv.   Where they had overcome an obstacle or kept going when things were difficult.

By focusing on the success they have achieved and increasing the positive to negative ratio of their self talk, you will begin to help create new habits in those students that need them. Greater confidence and self-esteem will follow.

2.  **Develop a positive learning culture in the classroom.** You can start by sharing an example, where you stepped out of your comfort zone and tried something new. This may have been difficult, but you did it anyway. Talk about the outcome. Show that when you learn something new you win, even if at first you don't get the outcome you want. It is making the effort that is the reward and if you keep working at it, you will make progress. Make this a regular part of your classroom ethos and show them that it is OK not to succeed at the first attempt, as long as you learn from the experience and keep going.

This book will build on these suggestions and share other ideas and choices, which will support you in building resilience and character in your students.

# CHAPTER TWO:
# THE BREADTH OF SUCCESS

Success is rather a vague term because it is subjective. Everyone has an opinion of what it is or is not, and if and when, they consider themselves to be successful. What one person thinks of as absolute success, another may consider poor, or even a failure!

Teaching young people that they can create their own definition of success, helps to build resilience. However, successful people do have common qualities and traits, which we explore in this chapter.

## Defining and Understanding Success

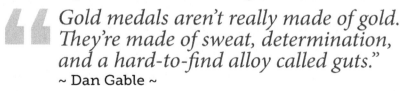

*Gold medals aren't really made of gold. They're made of sweat, determination, and a hard-to-find alloy called guts."*
~ Dan Gable ~

Success usually takes a great deal of personal effort, and achieving it without trying is rare and will probably be as a result of luck. Many people play the lottery each week, or look for other shortcuts to get what they want in life. By all means have some fun buying a ticket, but for nearly everyone, having this as their success plan or strategy, will end in disappointment. If success is to have true meaning, it needs to be won through hard work and determination.

To define your personal success criteria, you first need to understand yourself, your values, and your beliefs. What is it you stand for? Your values are *important* and may include such examples as respect, honesty, integrity, friendship, excellence, and hard work.

Values have a major *influence* on a person's *behaviour* and *attitude* and can serve as guidelines in life. They determine how you choose to behave. For example, if you show someone respect (value) you might demonstrate this by listening to them with care and attention (behaviour).

Part of defining what your success will look like, is to be able to see it in the future. You can achieve this through using visualisation. By thinking of your success as already having been achieved, and not as an aspiration or hope, and through making it vivid in your mind, you can create a powerful picture and positive emotions that will make your dreams seem real in the present moment. You will need to use your senses, being able to feel, see, and hear your success.

Answer the following two questions. You may want to make a note of your answers or write them down in full.

What does an ideal outcome look like for a specific goal you have?

Visualise what your ideal life looks like. This might include the job you have, where you live, your relationships, your lifestyle and everything else that is important to you.

Once you have a clear idea of your goal outcome or ideal life, you can compare this to where you are now and where you want to be.

Now plan for your success. Think about your ideal outcome or life and write down the specific steps that will help close the gap from where you are now. Part of this process is finding relevant knowledge, information, and people, which will help you on your journey. The steps need to be achievable and once your students begin to take and achieve them, it will build their confidence and resilience and help to overcome any self-limiting beliefs they may have.

Having set out the steps, you now need to take the action that will help you move towards your ideal outcome or life. For example, if you wish to be an artist, start drawing, or sketching every day and experience the joy that comes from pursuing something you are passionate about. Many people talk about dreams, but haven't got the clarity about what it is they want to achieve. You need to identify this and then every day, make sure your behaviours and actions are congruent to deliver what you want. We see so many people being constantly distracted, allowing others to sabotage their time or taking action that just does not fit with achieving their stated aims. Make sure this isn't you!

It's sometimes easier for children to grasp these concepts than for adults and it's exciting to watch children become engaged when they imagine what they'd like to do immediately or in the future. As a teacher, or parent, you can help them create their own success road map by focusing on:

- What they enjoy doing most.
- What their real interests are.
- What personal choices (goals) they need to make.
- What preparation, learning, and practise they need to do.
- What their success criteria will be, what obstacles

and challenges they might face, and how they will overcome them.

- What support they might need and who will help them.

Answering these will help you and your students navigate a path to success. It's a universal formula that works for all those who want to succeed.

## Skills, Attitudes and Qualities Linked to Success

Successful people have a range of attributes and qualities (which we share below). Take a few minutes to review each one and think about how they may help you and your students become more successful.

**Confidence:** To understand that you have the potential to succeed. To have self talk, which says 'I can do it' and 'I will give it a go' and to be comfortable in taking appropriate risks. You realise that there is no such thing as failure, only feedback. If you don't succeed at first in achieving the outcome you want, learn from the experience and try again. This attitude will make you stronger and more resilient.

**Commitment:** There is value in committing time and energy to achieving what you desire. It shows that you are dedicated and that it's important to take the time to plant and nurture the seeds of your future success. You may already have noticed that when you do what you really love, it doesn't feel like hard work, because it's your passion and so committing to action is easier.

**Leading others:** Successful people achieve their goals through leading others. Although it comes more easily to some people, leadership can be learned. The real secret of leading others is to engage them so that your agenda and theirs align. If they win, you win.

**Self-leadership:** When you look in the mirror you need to see someone who is successful, self-motivated and who is taking steps every day to make their dreams real. The first stage of self-leadership is self-awareness. Once you are aware of your own emotions, needs, desires and talents, you can then respond to the world with resourcefulness and resolve.

**Communication:** When you've connected with who you truly are and are clear about your message, you can share it with the world. Your ability to master presenting and talking, becomes an essential part of that process. When you are clear about your vision and values and plan carefully, you will be able to overcome any fears and deliver your message.

**Teamwork:** There are no one-man shows in life, and working and communicating in a team will support you to achieve success. Every leader needs their support team and as the acronym says, TEAM = Together Everyone Achieves More.

**Support team:** Your support team listens to your ideas, helps you stay focused when you may be straying off course, and encourages you when you have a difficult day. While every day isn't perfect, it is an opportunity to learn, make progress, and is a chance to test your resilience. Without support, you are unlikely to achieve the results you want and you only need to look at the world of professional sport, to see how athletes build success with their support team.

**Enjoyment:** Successful people enjoy what they do. The motivation that the enjoyment brings energises them and enables them to drive for success.

**Coaching:** Many successful people have or have had a coach, mentor, or inspiring teacher at some point in their lives; someone who helped to show them that they had potential that could be developed. Successful people regard those who coach them with gratitude and appreciation; and often look for the opportunity to share their knowledge with others; in recognition of the help, they have been given.

It's also interesting to note that in education, the word coaching is often linked with remedial work, while in business and sport it is the most successful and highest paid performers that often have a coach!

**Awareness and responsibility:** Successful people are both self-aware and personally responsible; they have the ability to respond with action and commitment to achieve their dreams.

**Dream big:** Never set a ceiling on your success and what you can achieve. Dreaming big is exciting, but not nearly as exciting as acting on those dreams and taking steps to achieve them. If you wish to sail the world, for example, you must first visualise yourself doing it, then begin the journey by learning how to sail.

**Humility:** Everyone needs to believe in themselves, but some people begin to think that they know it all and become egotistical or arrogant. Nobody can possibly know everything and most people recognise that they are on a journey of learning and discovery about themselves and the world around them. When we aren't prepared to be humble and learn from others, we can lose valuable insights that come from other's opinions and a different perspective.

Each one of the skills and qualities mentioned above doesn't cost anything to develop. All it takes is a desire to learn and a commitment to give the appropriate time, energy and focus. Learning these skills is often a process of trial and error, where you have to try new things in order to find out what works for you.

*Each one of the skills and qualities mentioned above doesn't cost anything to develop. All it takes is a desire to learn and a commitment to give the appropriate time, energy and focus.*

# CHAPTER THREE:
# THE SEVEN STEPS – NUMBER 1 PLACE

## Your Comfort Zone: Putting Yourself in the Place of Greatest Opportunity

*You have to be uncomfortable in order to be successful, in some ways. If you stay in your comfort zone you would never do the things that you need to do."*
~ Lights Poxleitner ~

**One day you will thank me for this.**

A comfort zone is a place where people feel most comfortable. It is a place where you feel safe, where you don't feel pushed and where you don't usually have high expectations placed on you. It's understandable not to try new things that may cause anxiety or fear. Yet by playing safe, we don't grow, and develop and just stay the same or even worse go backwards. By not trying new things and overcoming obstacles, we never have the opportunity to build resilience.

When you do step out of your comfort zone, you learn the joy that comes from taking risks, making progress, and being successful. This may be uncomfortable at first, but with each effort it becomes easier and as you grow in confidence and strength, you are able to meet more challenges.

Imagine that today you are standing on a cliff, looking down. You're getting ready to hang-glide for the first time, and your nerves are on edge. Even yesterday, you wouldn't have imagined yourself ever doing this. You are no thrill seeker. You're practical and grounded. Now, you're staring over that cliff, feeling the crisp wind on your face, and you're as scared as you can be. Yet, you've never felt more alive. There's that part of you that's feeling adventurous, shouting, "I want to do this!" Then there's that other part of you saying, "You're mad. That's what you are. Get away from the cliff now and go back home. I'll never mention it again." It would be so much easier to listen to that second voice – the one that has prevented you doing things in the past. However, there's something inside you that knows, you need to take that step off the cliff and whether it's difficult or not, you are excited.

What do you do? Do you take the jump, guided by the person who's done this hundreds of times and lived to tell the tale and share the experience? Alternatively, do you let yourself be ruled by that frightened voice in your head? With courage, you have a go and show that you can overcome your fears.

With the guide's encouragement and knowledge, you try it. You go running off that cliff and launch into the air. Before you know it, you are flying and you're looking at the world down below you. The perspective is amazing, and you are thrilled that you've done it and elated with the experience you've just had. When you land on the ground, it's almost disheartening. You want more. That is what stepping out of your comfort zone does. It turns your fears into your triumphs.

## Learning Outcomes

What do we learn about 'comfort zones'? In the last example, by having the courage to try something new, the person had a great learning experience. It may be that hang-gliding will not be a long-term passion for them (or something you want to try), but it was important for them to stretch themselves and try something new. By exploring different activities, it helps you find what does interest you and also builds your resilience to face any new challenges.

## Barriers versus Benefits

So what is it that stops someone from stepping out of their comfort zone and what are the benefits if they do?

Short of a true physical threat, the benefits are always likely to outweigh the barriers. The barriers can be debilitating, often leaving people feeling frustrated and disempowered. Some of the most obvious ones include:

*Fear of failure, lack of opportunity; self-limiting beliefs; lack of confidence; negative peer feedback; risk-averse culture; blind spots; lack of motivation; and apathy.*

It is genuinely sad when someone allows these barriers to overcome the real potential for growth and increased happiness that come from trying new experiences.  Some of the benefits of stepping out of a comfort zone are:

*Increased enjoyment; greater satisfaction; new knowledge; new opportunities; finding what you are good at; a sense of meaning and purpose; more energy; achievement; personal growth; empowerment; performance; creativity; enhanced learning; self- leadership and enhanced resilience.*

It is a great gift to give a child the opportunity to step into their achievement zone.  This is the first step to building resilience – starting from the right **place**.  Not only will they ignite sparks of enthusiasm in their own lives but also they will hopefully inspire others to follow their example and experience everything that life has to offer.

How does a person learn to step outside their comfort zone? There are some simple ideas that will help them:

1) **Win/lose versus win/learn**

   Most people operate on a win/lose basis.  You see it in sport, business and within your everyday lives.  You try something and win or lose, succeed or fail.  The press or media don't help, often showing people to be heroes or villains.  There seems to be little middle ground.

   There is often a lot of negative emotion and publicity (even if it is just in front of friends) associated with trying something new, with the possibility of being seen as a failure or loser.

   It is more helpful to focus on developing a win/learn mindset.  When you try something new, you will know what result you want, but you don't always achieve it on the first attempt.  It may be a better or worse result than you would have liked and the important lesson is to adopt an attitude, which says you might have (failed) this time, but what did you learn and how can you use this in trying again? The important questions to ask are, "What did I learn from the experience?" and "What would I do differently next time?"

Creating a positive win/learn mindset removes negative emotion and the fear of failure. It does take practise to make this an everyday habit, but once you change your thinking, you will wonder why you ever found it so difficult to try new things.

2) Recognise what is holding you back. It is usually a lack of confidence, or a fear of some sort (failure or ridicule). Try to put it in perspective. Ask what the worst thing that can happen is if you try this and it doesn't quite work first time. Link it with win/learn.

3) Create a mantra for yourself so that when your self talk says things like 'I can't' or 'this will be difficult', you can replace these with the words such as 'I can' or 'I want to have a go'.

4) Identify the benefits of taking a risk. How will it help you to achieve the things you want? How will it help you grow as a person? As an exercise, you can discuss this with friends or in the classroom.

5) It is also powerful to visualise success. See yourself being successful in the future, as if it were already true now. Make your vision real by using all your senses, for example 'seeing what you are doing, hearing people say good things about you and feeling the excitement in what you are achieving'.

6) Young people develop habits more easily than adults do, and they don't have to unlearn old habits and thought patterns. Showing them how to create new habits is empowering and it will help them fulfil their potential. That shy girl can be the lead in the school play. That introverted boy can be a passionate speaker about a subject that inspires him.

7) Thinking about the benefits and strategies of stepping out of your comfort zone, will raise the likelihood of you taking action. As a teacher, share your own stories with students. Be a good role model by admitting that at times you were scared, but took on challenges anyway. Tell them about the insights and learning gained from your experiences.

Expanding your abilities and interests usually means stepping outside your comfort zone. What better way for a child to do that, than with a guiding hand from a respected teacher, parent, or adult?

## Success Stories

Think about famous people, world-class athletes or people you know and you admire. What do you think made them a role model or special for you? You will probably have observed that they had a passion for their particular activity; they took action

*Think about famous people, world-class athletes or people you know and you admire. What do you think made them a role model or special for you?*

and they never gave up as they moved towards their dreams. Their stories will undoubtedly also show how they stepped out of their comfort zones and how they overcame fears, obstacles and major setbacks.

One story that shows incredible courage and perseverance comes from Darren Campbell MBE, an Olympic Gold Medal winning athlete from the UK and now a successful businessman and somebody we have worked with. He grew up in a neighbourhood that was less than ideal, challenged by both poverty and gangs and living on a tough estate with his single mum. It would have been easy for him to accept his lot and perhaps follow a negative path.

Two events changed his outlook on life. Firstly, when he was 11 years old he watched Carl Lewis, the US sprinter, win four gold medals at the 1984 Olympics in Los Angeles, and secondly he walked past some grand houses on his way to school, and thought that one day he would like to live in one of those. Therefore, he made two commitments to himself,

He was going to win a gold medal and he wanted to own a large house. He decided it was okay for him to dream big. This is a message he gives to young people today, encouraging them to follow their dreams (irrespective of their start in life, or their current circumstances), even if other people might not think it possible.

Darren made his dreams real, by actually saying them out loud and even went around, aged 12, practicing signing his autograph. He told people of his ambition and received plenty of laughter and criticism for his ideas. Others didn't understand, but he knew that he had to make his claim in order for it to happen. He began to put all his energy into sport and as a result, his academic performance suffered. His mother, who wanted to ensure he had a good education, cut back the sports he could participate in, until he improved his grades, which he did. It seemed like everything was on track, but even with his commitment, Darren did end up falling into the gang culture of his neighbourhood.

Most would have thought he had given up his dreams and reverted to what was 'expected of him', but Darren didn't give up that easily. Like many people, he just needed a reminder of why his goals were important and what the consequences would be if he didn't step out of his current life. That reminder came when a friend was murdered from gang related violence. So as a young man he took a significant step and uprooted his life, moving away, wanting to separate himself from the gangs to pursue his dream.

It was then that the magic began to happen. After much dedication and perseverance, Darren did earn that gold medal. At first though, he had some difficult setbacks from injuries and at his very first Olympics, he dropped the baton in the 4 x 100 metres relay race, for which he received a lot of criticism from the press.

Yet, he didn't give up because he was driven by his dream of winning a gold medal. He kept stepping out of his comfort zone and putting himself in the places of most opportunity for his career. He truly built great resilience and today, in his talks to young people, he says

 *Never ever ever give up on your dreams."*

His message is if you persevere and are prepared to work hard, you can achieve anything. He now lives in a big house in Wales.

Darren's story is quite inspirational and one that shows the true heart of a champion. He did three important things to help him achieve his dream:

- He didn't accept the environment he was born into as the limit of what he could achieve.

- He claimed what he wanted and didn't let the lack of support dissuade him.

- He took courageous steps to separate himself from what was holding him back.

This type of inspiration doesn't stop at Darren Campbell.

Before Walt Disney made his mark, cartoons at theatres were simply animated shorts. Walt saw potential for much more – an entire animated story. People told him he was crazy and that financing it would be a poor investment. Adults wouldn't want to go and see a full-length cartoon.

How wrong were those people! When Walt Disney released Snow White, moviegoers were immediately enchanted by the classic tale turned into a full-length animated movie. He kept pursuing his creative vision. In fact, his motto was, 'Keep Moving Forward'. And keep moving forward he did.

Walt's dream to bring out the child in everyone, extended beyond the silver screen. He created Disneyland, a place where all his stories came to life and where families were able to interact with the characters. What an ideal vacation. Walt extended his vision further, wanting to create Disney World in Florida.

Roy Disney, Walt's brother, frowned at the idea, but Walt knew he must try. It would be worth it. This began a long process of secretly buying land (because people would automatically attach more zeros to swampland in Florida, if they knew that the 'man behind the mouse' was responsible for the purchase). The result is a magical and amazing place for people to visit, something that was built on imagination and the motivation and vision of one man.

We all have the ability of Walt Disney, to have creative ideas and be inspired by our passions. It's up to us to take the chances and work towards making those ideas a reality. It takes passion, vision, and action – and in Walt's case, a desire to keep moving forward and not allowing others to hold him back. His is a great example of what one man can create if he takes a risk and commits to his dreams.

## Thought Momentum

What place do you find yourself in today? Hopefully, it is a place where you know that you've taken risks, and aren't left saying to yourself 'if only'.

If you're like many people, you might have wished someone had encouraged you more, providing words that inspired you to act and not remain stationary. As a teacher how rewarding is it to let a young person know that it is okay to try something, even if at first it may feel uncomfortable.

Sometimes as a teacher, you need to believe in them first, before they believe in themselves. It can start simply by asking questions that stimulate their thinking and encourages them to dream of new ideas and adventures. All young people are naturally curious and want to enjoy life and perform. It sometimes takes a little help to give them the confidence to take their first step.

## Taking the Next Step

One way to share these ideas with your students is to open up with a story or experience in which you learned a valuable lesson. Bring out the learning in what happened to you and in how they can benefit. You can do this by:

1. Sharing your experience.

2. Asking the students about their experiences.

3. Asking what they might have done differently.

You may have to encourage them to talk at first, as some might be shy or fearful. Perhaps they could share ideas in pairs or small groups before discussing in a plenary.

To help them take these ideas on to another level, you might ask them to create a story about their own future or create fictional characters and do the same. Give them a few guidelines to help make the project easier and stimulate their thinking. Some things they could consider are:

1. What is their dream/vision and why is it exciting to them?

2. Where will they go on their journey?

3. What things may happen, as they pursue their dreams and ideas?

4. How will they start?

5. What obstacles will they face and how will they overcome them?

6. How will they finish?

7. Who will help them?

8. When and how will they know they have achieved their goal?

Those eight elements can help create a good story. While it may be fictional or real, it will have planted seeds of genuine possibilities in their minds. You cannot help but be inspired, when you approach your story in this way; imagining yourself in it as it unfolds and feeling like you've truly lived the experience by the time it is ended. You could also ask your students to draw or paint a picture of their ideas, to appeal to those who prefer to express themselves visually rather than in writing. The result will be equally rewarding.

You can also link comfort zones with a conversation around change. Change brings out a number of emotions in people, both positive and negative. Some thrive on it, some go with the flow, and other more fearful people resist it every step of the way. It's natural to feel different emotions at some point in your life, and it might be good to explore the following.

What has been your student's personal experience of change? How do they feel about change, bringing out both positive and negative feelings? You might consider factors such as; why is change exciting or frightening? What are the benefits of embracing change? What might help you through a period of change? What is one thing (within your control) that you might want to change today?

End the discussion with students by asking each of them to give one action they will take immediately, to make one change they want. The idea will hopefully take them out of their comfort zone and help them start a journey of positive change. Do follow this up later and ask students to share their experiences of making the change. The stories of those that succeed or adopt a win/learn attitude will support and encourage all students to take further steps.

Finally act as a role model. You cannot expect your students to make these changes if your behaviour isn't congruent.

Sometimes you might hear yourself say out loud, "I can't do that", or "I don't want to do it." This might be for example, if you are asked to speak in an assembly or to a large group, or any number of things that are outside your comfort zone. Do not underestimate the power of example, as actions really do speak louder than words and showing that you can conquer your fear and step out of your comfort zone, will really support your students in their progress.

Step one to building resilience is to put yourself in the <u>place</u> of most opportunity!

> *We haven't failed. We know a thousand things won't work so we're that much closer to finding what will."*
> ~ Thomas Edison ~

*Do not underestimate the power of example, as actions really do speak louder than words and showing that you can conquer your fear and step out of your comfort zone, will really support your students in their progress.*

# CHAPTER FOUR:
# THE SEVEN STEPS - NUMBER 2 PASSION

> *There is no passion to be found playing small, in settling for a life that is less than the one you are capable of living."*
> ~ Nelson Mandela ~

Passion comes from the heart and you generate it when you have a true interest in a subject or activity. Passion gives you the positive energy that enables you to drive towards achieving your vision and goals. Passion gives you the tenacity to do things that might seem difficult, because you realise they are important to you personally.

People remember individuals who are passionate. There is something about them that draws you to them like a magnet. You become curious about their story, perhaps a bit envious of their happiness and success, and wonder if you can have such enthusiasm in your life (if you don't already).

Yet all people have passion and are capable of being fulfilled. You just need to find those things that ignite your interest. When you find and unlock your passion, you will have the energy and drive to overcome any obstacles in life and be resilient. If you are not sure how to find your passion here are some things to think about.

- Self-awareness (who are you and what do you want)?
- What types of things/activities have given you enjoyment in the past?
- What really excites you?
- What activities might you like to try?
- Who has inspired you, what was your interest in them and what did they do?

*All people have passion and are capable of being fulfilled. You just need to find those things that ignite your interest.*

In our hearts, we all understand what makes us passionate. Young people often show their enthusiasm more easily than adults do, but we all have it. Teachers have the opportunity to explore this with young people and help them find what really motivates them.

Motivational speakers often share stories where people's passion and commitment, have overcome huge challenges and have produced great achievements. Susan Boyle is a good example; she auditioned for Britain's Got Talent, something that was also well outside her comfort zone.

At first, as she walked out on stage, everyone seemed to look at her and wonder what she could possibly be doing there. She smiled, not allowing the audience to put her off and proceeded to sing 'I Dreamed a Dream', which made even the tough Simon Cowell's jaw drop in amazement. She was incredible and there was no denying her passion for singing as she showed Britain, and later the world, her talent. You (or your students) may not have the same singing talent as Susan Boyle, but you have the opportunity of finding your passion and what makes your heart sing.

## Learning Outcomes

Through thoughtful discussions, teachers can help their students explore what gives them enjoyment, inspiration and passion.

Helping students to find their passion will give them a great start in life, instead of them wandering aimlessly without direction. As a teacher, you can inspire through action.

1) Realise that success flows more easily when you enjoy what you are doing. In life it is important to make conscious choices about who you are, what really

interests you and where you want to focus your time and energy?

2) Understand that the more aware you are of what inspires you and the choices available to you, the higher the chances of achieving success. Many people become disillusioned with life, because they can't find what they want to do. Trying out different activities and areas of study is an essential part of finding your passion.

## High Energy and Positive Emotions

When people are passionate, they find themselves in a state of high energy and positive emotion. It is also true that everyone, whether adult or child, feeds off each other's moods and emotions. Whether your emotions are positive or negative, they have a direct impact on how people respond to you, at home, as well as at school. While you cannot always control how you feel, you can control and manage how you respond to people, situations, and events.

Let's examine two emotional categories:

- Negative
- Positive

We all have emotions; some will be positive and some negative and you can see these in the above table. Successful people manage their emotions by focusing their attention mainly on positive high energy. Of course they can't stay in this state all the time, so they allow themselves sufficient downtime to relax and recover in a state of peace and tranquillity (positive low energy). They generally live their lives on the right-hand side of the above grid. Our ability to focus on this side is helped when we are passionate and interested in life.

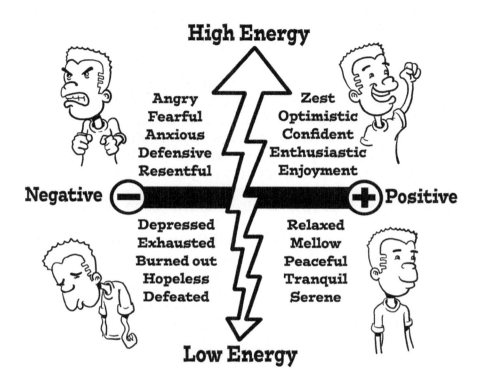

We can have high energy that is charged with negative emotions. This is not very helpful and includes traits such as Anger, Fear, Anxiety, Defensiveness, and Resentfulness.

Alternatively, we can have high energy that is charged with positive emotions. This is preferable because it is much more productive and includes a Zest for life, Optimism, Confidence, Enthusiasm, and Enjoyment.

Not everybody shows their emotions, regardless of how they are feeling. Many people prefer to be quiet and not be noticed, although it doesn't mean that they don't feel these positive (or negative) emotions.

There are also people who have negative emotions and low energy, and they might exhibit traits like Depression, Exhaustion, Burnout, Hopelessness, and Defeat.

You can often identify these negative emotions by the way a person looks and behaves. For example their body language with head down, shrugged shoulders and little eye contact. This often happens when young people are struggling in some aspect of their life, particularly when it comes to identifying who they truly are and what they might want out of life.

There are also people whose natural state is more laid-back and relaxed (low energy but positive) and I'm sure that you have students and friends who are like this. They demonstrate the following traits: Relaxed, Mellow, Peaceful, Tranquil, and Serene.

There is a possible downside with this state, as they may not make enough effort to find their passion or to overcome setbacks. It is by putting yourself in a place of high energy and positive attitude, that you are able to drive to achieve great results.

However, for those who are positive and have high energy, finding time to relax and think can be extremely beneficial. For elite athletes, preparation and recovery time is very important, if they want to perform consistently at their best. The same is true for all of us, if we want to be at the top of our game. So providing quiet reflection time for short periods, as some schools do, can help young people.

Trying to show students how to generate positive energy and to make good choices sounds fairly challenging, doesn't it? Yet, it is something that you've probably used to support your teaching in the past. Think of scenarios where you have injected your own positive energy and seen results such as:

- Seeing the smile on a child's face after they overcame a challenging problem, which had been so difficult for them.

- Getting that quiet student to a stage where they felt courageous enough to speak up in class.

- Receiving the coveted thank you at the end of a class, along with a genuine smile of appreciation.

- Getting progress reports on your past students as they succeed and knowing that you played a small part in their development.

Positive changes usually happen one student at a time, but can be contagious. You can be the teacher who inspires their students by helping them find their passion. Young people also learn through the example of others and sharing success stories.

## Success Stories

Stories that inspire us are often based on someone's passion to make a change, make a difference, or pursue an interest despite what others may say.

One such story is that of James Corden, a very successful writer and actor. He was a boisterous child, the kind that drives many teachers to distraction. As a result, many had written him off as someone who would constantly make a nuisance of himself. James didn't see it that way.

Where they saw disruption, he wanted to bring laughter front and centre and to be centre stage. It started when he was seven and he received a role in his school's play. He enjoyed it so much that he wanted to learn more about acting, and his parents enrolled him in the Jackie Palmer Stage School, an after school acting and dancing program.

James immediately loved being on stage. He could focus easily on learning lines, and everybody really liked him. It gave him tremendous enjoyment, while so many other school subjects didn't hold his interest.

He'd go to many auditions, attending at least one a week. Yet, he didn't get a role. Trying to be kind to him, people said that he should give up on his dream of being an actor. James didn't listen though. It was his passion and he really wanted to do it.

Committed to seeing it through, he kept improving, learning the lessons from his 'failures', and working smarter and harder. Many would have given up, but not James. Even his dad, who took him to the auditions every week, wanted him to give up, as he didn't want to see more disappointment on James' face. Then one day it finally happened, he got a role in a West End show in London, as a member of the chorus. He had one line to speak, but he'd earned that line. He was seventeen years old. That role was the reward for his years of dedication and his passion for acting and it was also just the start.

James subsequently starred in a sitcom that he co-wrote, created a key figure that supported comic relief's efforts and won the coveted Tony award for best actor in a Broadway play. Today he is a familiar face on television and he is living his dream. None of that would have been possible, if he hadn't seen how passion makes hard work, and yes some heartache, worth it.

Acting and writing careers are very tough to get into and his story illustrates the success that comes from passion and determination. It also helps you realise what can happen when you have real conviction and are prepared to follow through. There may be *lights* and a *camera*, but the movie of your life doesn't happen, without you finding what you enjoy doing. Unfortunately, many people never find the one thing at which they would have excelled.

Another success story is that of Amy Tan. It's sometimes difficult to change careers when you are already successful and many people just stick with what they know. Amy Tan didn't subscribe to that way of thinking.

Amy worked for a technical writing business with a partner and although it was writing, something she loved, it wasn't the writing she really wanted to do. Going out and meeting clients, doing cost estimates, and having billable hours, which were all part of her job, didn't really inspire her.

Amy was the daughter of immigrants and she wanted to show the world how she could express herself through the English language, which she had learned in the technical writing field. She asked her employer if she could do more writing, but was told that it wasn't really her strength. Estimates and collecting bills were.

Not able to come to an agreement with her employer, Amy quit her job. She knew that if she wanted to pursue her dream, she had to focus her time and energy on writing. Knowing that a writer doesn't go from broke to multimillionaire overnight (hint: J.K. Rowling), Amy began to do freelance work in technical writing, while working on the ideas for her novels. She put in long days and nights, fully committed to figuring out how to pay the bills and pursue her passion.

Amy ended up writing bestsellers including, *The Joy Luck Club.* She may have been termed a technical writer at first, but that was just a technicality. She showed a true mastery of fiction, with a captivating story that really brought her into a whole new career, one that was based on her passion. She was wise not to take no for an answer and to never give up on her dream, a lesson that we can all learn.

## Thought Momentum

Being passionate about what you do, helps in the following areas:

*Motivation, Excitement, Enjoyment, Work Ethic, and Dedication.*

As a teacher, you are no doubt passionate about your life and have many exciting messages to share with your students. They will listen to you when they realise that you are genuine and motivated to help them succeed. You don't have to be a powerful speaker or polished presenter to do it either (although many teachers do excel at this).

The formula for success is simple. It just entails leading by example:

*Sharing your passions creates a chain affect, in which others will want to pursue theirs.*

If you haven't thought about it for a while, take some time to think about what made you passionate about teaching and helping young people.

## Taking the Next Step

Showing young people how to pinpoint what they are passionate about and to act on their best interests, is a good starting point. Here are some areas that will help them to do this.

### Awareness

There are times when the things you are most passionate about may not be clear to you and it is even truer for young people. Sometimes it's easier for others to see it rather than you. Here are ways to unlock your passion.

- Make a list of what you enjoy doing most and say why.

- Take a moment to reflect on how certain activities made you feel at the time you were doing them.

- Exclude things that you think you must do and focus on the activities that you genuinely enjoy.

Ask your students to consider each of these in turn and also how they might develop some of the following traits, where needed.

## Confidence

Confidence enables us to pursue our passions even when we fear failure or setbacks. When we have confidence, we have a positive mindset and we see the opportunities in everything that happens in life. It helps build resilience, because when people don't get the results they want, they don't have to take it too personally or negatively.

## Persistence

William Edward Hickson is a British educator who is credited with popularising the proverb: *If at first you don't succeed, try, try, and try again.* Persistence or never giving up is a quality that supports everyone, every day, in achieving their goals.

If your passions and interests are to be not just personally fulfilling, but sustainable, they need to be underpinned by positive values. Pursuing a passion cannot be something that is harmful or detrimental to others.

## Honesty

Passion underpins your desire to succeed. However, you must be honest with yourself. You may have great dreams but the acid test is whether you are prepared to put in the hard work and dedication to achieve your goals.

In Darren Campbell's story he dreamed of being an Olympian and was honest with himself in understanding that he needed to change his way of life (not being in a gang), in order to be successful. He also realised that it would take a great deal of personal effort and commitment, to be able to stand on the podium with a gold medal around his neck.

### Enjoyment
Not everything is enjoyable 100% of the time, but when you are doing something you are passionate about, even the seemingly boring parts can be endured. When you ask your students to think about why they enjoyed something, make sure it isn't just based on the most exciting parts. The football player spends a lot of hours practicing to become a professional. The candy maker cannot eat their products all the time. Astronauts spend many years in the classroom before they are allowed to take a flight into space.

### Support
Support is valuable in achieving any dream or goal. In fact, it is essential, because you often need other people to help you and it's good to have others to share your journey. Some of the most valued forms of support come from teachers, mentors, parents, friends and family.

This is because they give acknowledgement and recognition of your efforts and give encouragement in difficult times.

*Financial support can also play a part, but as a teacher you want your students to focus on the things that are within their control and don't necessarily cost money. Support them to make a commitment to take action.*

### Empathy
We may have our passions, but it's also good to understand others. Empathy is the ability to be able to place yourself in

another's shoes and understand what they are feeling and experiencing. Often it is when people are busy, that they are wrapped up in their own little worlds and don't notice what is happening around them. If you want others to help you, then you need to understand and support them too.

As an example, many people are critical of young people and their behaviour, particularly those who are not well behaved. Yet they don't often stop to think what their life is like and if they were in their shoes, how they would feel or behave.

Three ways to help students gain empathy for others are to:

- Teach them about the power of listening to others.
- Show them how to ask meaningful and searching questions.
- Help them to focus on being curious, open-minded, and non-judgemental.

When life gets tough and people face challenges, it is their values, such as honesty, enjoyment, support, and empathy, which help create resilience in their lives.

As a teacher, you can ask insightful questions that help your students think about their passions and interests. Questions such as:

> *"When life gets tough and people face challenges, it is their values, such as honesty, enjoyment, support, and empathy, which help create resilience in their lives."*

- *What do you like doing and what are your strengths?*
  They can do this in small groups or one on one with
  you. Ask your students to explore what makes them
  passionate. Most students will give a simple answer
  first, like video games. This may be one interest, but
  there's often more to their story. Explore and ask more
  questions. You may even want to do a questioning
  session with a student in front of the class, to give
  ideas to other students of how they can approach this.

- *What do you dislike doing and why?* This is a
  good question to ask because the answer will
  often reveal a lack of confidence in a particular
  area, which may prevent them from trying
  their best. In fact, if they found a way to get
  past it, it may even become a passion.

  We met a teacher who shared that they became a
  mathematics teacher, in order to help those young
  people who struggled to understand the subject.
  They'd gone through that experience themselves
  and had empathy for those students who felt it was
  just too difficult. It had just taken one interested
  teacher, who took the time to acknowledge that
  sometimes those mental blocks exist and who
  then made mathematics accessible for them.
  They now wanted to do the same for others.

- *Is there a step you can take to become better at
  doing something that challenges you?* Depending
  on the situation, you may find that students can
  easily overcome what they say is challenging, by
  devoting some time to it (either on their own or
  with the help of a friend, teacher, or in class).

End the session with at least one idea from every student
regarding what they can do to improve something with which

they currently struggle. To develop a passion for learning is a gift that all teachers can encourage.

At the end of discussions about self-improvement, it is important to talk about what students would like to try and why. You may find out that they are ready to try something new, but are just nervous to start. They may not be great at sports, but would love to try out a new activity. They may love to learn to ride, but are slightly nervous about getting on a horse. So help them think about what they need to do, to take the first step in following their new interest.

Don't forget to share what you'd like to try and how you're going to go about it too. Teachers have the ability to be great role models and set the tone with enthusiasm.

Step two to building resilience – find your passion to realise your potential.

 *Passion is energy. Feel the power that comes from focusing on what excites you."*
~ Oprah Winfrey ~

# CHAPTER FIVE:
# THE SEVEN STEPS – NUMBER 3 PURPOSE

*I think the purpose of life is to be useful,
to be responsible, to be compassionate.
It is, above all to matter, to count, to
stand for something, to  have made
some difference that you lived at all.*"
~ Leo Rosten ~

Purpose is the why or reason for doing something. It's what gives meaning to your life and is often linked to being of service to others. It's the drive to make a useful contribution, by using your unique talents and gifts. It may involve being part of something bigger than you, for example belonging to an organisation, group, or movement that wants to make a positive difference in the world.

Steve Jobs the founder of Apple was one individual who had a profound impact on the world. He was driven by the desire to challenge the status quo and to make sure every person was able to unlock their talent, by having easy access to innovative, efficient and beautiful computers and other technological products that would delight them. That was his personal drive and purpose and he carried it with him throughout his life.

Purpose is also connected with fulfilling your highest potential through tapping into your internal motivation, for example learning, enjoyment, and performance.

Knowing your purpose, gives you a sense of power and direction in life. It makes it much easier to create a plan that will help lead to your success. When you have purpose, you feel as if you are on a mission to achieve your own life goals and as a result, can overcome obstacles and develop the resilience that you'll need for your journey.

Most people want to have a sense of meaning and purpose and to know that they have something unique to offer the world, which will be appreciated by others and give them personal satisfaction.

It is linked to **"being the best you can be"**.

Adults sometimes lose their sense of purpose, or wake up realising that they aren't sure what it is for them. Young people have an advantage, because they can learn about purpose from teachers, parents and other role models.

Your purpose can also change as your life changes, because it aligns with growth, self-awareness, and self development. For example as you take on roles in life, such as being a teacher or parent or manager, your responsibilities change and this can directly affect your purpose.

You can identify your purpose by understanding:

- Who you are and what it is you stand for.

- What gives you a sense of fulfilment or satisfaction.

- What service you can give to others.

- What interest and abilities you might be able to utilise to make a difference.

- What you want to experience and learn in life.

- What lessons can be learned from other people's stories.

## Learning Outcomes

Finding your purpose will enable you to make clear decisions in your life as to what you do, what you want to experience, what you want to learn, and how you can grow through developing skills and being of service to others. When you find your purpose, two outcomes make it easier to move forward.

1) Your passion aligns with your purpose, to enable you not just to 'be the best you can be' but also to be the best for others too.

2) You are more able to create a plan, which uses your talents and strengths and you are therefore more likely to stick to it and deliver it.

Teachers can support and challenge young people to find their purpose and make the best of any situation or opportunity. It's important to realise that every young person has:

*Purpose, inspiration and dreams, a unique individuality, internal resources and talent, and a capacity to make a contribution.*

What they usually lack is the awareness of who they really are and what they can contribute. As a teacher, you can help them find their purpose and be the conduit that enables them to generate ideas and see them come to fruition?

## What Creates Purpose?

As a human being, you inherently have purpose, because life gives you the opportunity to learn, perform, and have enjoyment. However, it is more powerful if you can consciously choose a path that unlocks your purpose, by making choices linked to your dreams and aspirations. Understanding your talents and strengths, and knowing how to use them for the benefit of yourself and others, will then help you to fulfil this purpose.

Here are three questions that teachers can ask their students, to help them understand and develop their purpose:

1) What does having a purpose in life mean? It can be different for everyone and bring different results. These discussions are a good time to share ideas and may bring forward words and phrases such as, enjoyment, learning, motivation, sense of identity, having a sense of fulfilment, being of service, making a contribution, mission, and achieving important life goals.

2) How does having a clear purpose help? This is a significant question and one that is worthy of reflection. One answer to this question lies in empowerment. When you have a sense of purpose, it galvanises your thoughts and energy and enables you to focus on achieving a given outcome. It gives you a real sense of self-worth, knowing that you are making a contribution through using your unique talents.

3) Who have you met or read about who has lived or is living a purposeful life? People's success stories are often a good way of gaining insights and understanding – they may help us focus on our own lives and what it is we want.

Take a few minutes and see how you might define purpose in your life.

## Success Stories

**Nelson Rolihlahla Mandela** was born 18th July 1918 and died 5th December 2013. He was a man with a true mission and sense of purpose. He was born in South Africa at a time when apartheid (the segregation of white and black people) was the norm.

Nelson trained as a lawyer and his dream was that all men, whatever their colour, race or religion, would be free and live as equals. In his autobiography 'A Long Walk to Freedom', he tells the story of how he, together with many others, fought to change the system of apartheid.

His quest didn't come without great sacrifice and he served 27 years in prison, initially on Robben Island, and later in Pollsmoor Prison and Victor Verster Prison for his activities to bring about change.

However, he persevered and brought about the changes he sought and served as President of South Africa from 1994 to 1999. He was South Africa's first black chief executive, and the first elected in a fully representative democratic election. His government focused on dismantling the legacy of apartheid, through tackling institutionalised racism, poverty, and inequality, and fostering racial reconciliation.

Mandela retired after one term in office and became an elder statesman, focusing on charitable work in combating poverty and HIV/AIDS through the Nelson Mandela Foundation.

Here was a man of great integrity and courage, who had a sense of who he was foremost as a human being and who had the right to express himself and live in freedom. His desire for this was not just for himself, but also for all of humanity. He empowered himself and others to bring about great change in the country he loved, South Africa, and he is an example of what can be achieved when you truly find and live your purpose.

### Richard Branson

Richard Branson, the founder of Virgin, has made it his mission to empower people through building successful businesses. He wasn't born with the skills to create eight different multimillion dollar organisations, in eight different countries. It took a lot of work, dedication, and an acknowledgement; that you must not only find your strengths, but also find people who can support you in your areas of weakness. That was something that he didn't learn in school, but gained through experience.

Branson is the first to admit that his teachers didn't think he was too brilliant and that he was a dreamer. He was dyslexic and not particularly engaged in schoolwork. At the time, he didn't really understand his purpose, although his teachers could see that he had potential. He needed to find something that interested him. When he graduated from school, the headmaster commented that he'd either end up in prison, or be a millionaire. Branson thought, "He's right." That was his motivation to become an entrepreneur.

When he left school, his days of dreaming were put to good use as he started to put his ideas into action. He knew it would be scary and difficult at times to achieve his aims, but he believed he could do it. It all came down to being brave enough to be different.

At the age of sixteen, his first business venture was a magazine called Student. In 1970, he set up a mail order record business. In 1972, he opened a chain of record stores, Virgin Records, much later to become Virgin Megastores. Branson's Virgin brand grew rapidly during the 1980s, as he set up Virgin Atlantic and expanded the Virgin Records music label. According to the Forbes 2012 list of billionaires, Branson was the sixth richest citizen of the United Kingdom, at that time, with an estimated net worth of US$4.6 billion.

Richard Branson has also used his success to help create greater meaning for himself and others, through his humanitarian activities. For example, in the late 1990s, Branson and musician Peter Gabriel discussed with Nelson Mandela their idea of a small, dedicated group of leaders, working objectively and without any vested personal interest to solve difficult global conflicts. On 18th July 2007, in Johannesburg, South Africa, Nelson Mandela announced the formation of a new group, The Elders, sponsored by Branson and Gabriel. The Elders use their collective skills to catalyse peaceful resolutions to long-standing conflicts, articulate new approaches to global issues that are causing human suffering, and share wisdom by helping to connect voices all over the world. Once your purpose is clear and powerful, it can lead to extraordinary acts and provide the resilience to ensure you are able to fulfil them.

## Visualisation

We have already mentioned visualisation and it is a powerful tool that we promote and repeat in the book. When people find their purpose, they often use visualisation as a powerful technique to help them create the future that they want. Actors, athletes, business and school leaders, and teachers we know, all use it to help them make their dreams a reality.

An example. One of the best tennis players ever, Roger Federer is known for his incredible physical prowess and ability to sense the next shot, without having to think too much about it. This isn't coincidence or some form of hidden ability. According to Federer, he implanted mental imagery (visualisation) into his training regime.

He imagined performing at a high level on the tennis court. He incorporates this technique into his life when he is on and off the court. The result is that he is prepared for the tough competition and is confident that he can achieve success because he's played it out in his mind so many times. This includes matches before he plays them. The result is an impressive record, which includes some of the highest achievements of any tennis player. As of September 2014, he had achieved the most grand slam titles at 17; the most grand slam finals at 24; and 10 consecutive appearances in the final matches for a grand slam title. The list could go on for quite a while, but you get the idea. He's great at what he does and he doesn't leave his success to chance.

If you want to be successful and experience what your purpose could look like, you would be well served by using positive mental imagery (visualisation). That is seeing yourself acting out your purpose though using your imagination.

Visualisation gave Federer the opportunity to prepare mentally to achieve his dreams and goals. Of course, it didn't prevent him from losing at times, but allowed him to focus his mind on what he could influence. His personal resilience was built on knowing that he was well prepared, that he could learn from his mistakes and losses and could come back even stronger.

## Thought Momentum

As a teacher, you can help your students work on their purpose. Here are some ways that you can be of support.

- Help them find what inspires them.

- Help them understand what activities might have meaning for them.

- Help them realise what is important or not important in their life.

- Help them see that making a contribution or helping others, can give a sense of purpose.

- Help them see how defining purpose is a driver for their success.

Understanding the reasons why we do something provides us with the mental and emotional strength to move forward. Having purpose not only enables us to grow, but by being of service to others, we can make a real contribution to the world. Teachers in particular have purpose naturally woven into their work, as they serve their students every day.

Through your ability to open young people's minds you can show them that their purpose can:

- Empower them and give them a sense of direction.

- Make it easier to create plans that lead to success.

- Conquer obstacles and build resilience.

- Offer their special gifts to the world.

- Be a role model for others.

As a teacher, you can see their strengths and abilities. If you show them how to combine their personal interests with being of service to others, you help them find purpose in life.

## Taking the Next Step

You can have an interesting conversation with your students and find their level of understanding using the following three sections.

There are three steps to this first section.

1) Ask your students what having a purpose means. You may have to guide them by sharing:

- Purpose involves learning and experiencing life.

- Purpose includes doing things that are interesting and important to them.

- Purpose is often found by developing their skills and abilities.

- Purpose includes being of service to others, as well as yourself.

- Purpose is about being the best you can be.

2) In pairs or small groups, ask your students to discuss why having a clear purpose is important. Some of the answers may include the following:

*Clarity, direction, understanding, meaning, fulfilment, freedom, choice, responsibility, learning, motivation, joy, contribution, service to others, developing interests and skills and performing.*

3) Discuss examples of people who live purposeful lives - these might be national figures or people you know locally. This can be done as a class or in small groups. Through discussion highlight that all these people:

- Understand their purpose.
- Realise their potential through learning and personal growth.
- Develop their skills and knowledge.
- Respond positively to life's challenges.
- Are of service and making a difference in other people's lives.

The second section involves students tapping into their own interests and purpose. This exercise is in two parts.

**Part 1:**

Generating ideas around what their purpose might be.

You may want to suggest a list to discuss when they talk about their individual purpose. The list might include:

- What do they think their own purpose might be?
- Why do they get excited about that purpose?
- What interests and skills might it include?
- How does their purpose help others as well as themselves?

## Part 2:

Create specific ideas to get started.  Questions for them to consider are:

- What research do they need to do to find their purpose?
- Who might it be good to talk with?
- What knowledge, skills, and qualities would they like to develop?
- How could they develop a route map for their life?

The third section about purpose is putting it all together. Students can write their own story of success, incorporating their purpose, as well as people, interests, skills, qualities, learning and other activities.  Alternatively, they can draw a picture, which captures their life story.

Step three of building resilience – determining your purpose!

 *Everyone has his own specific vocation or mission in life; everyone must carry out a concrete assignment that demands fulfilment.  Therein he cannot be replaced, nor can his life be repeated.  Thus, everyone's task is unique as is his specific opportunity to implement it."*
~ Viktor E. Frankl, Man's Search for Meaning ~

# CHAPTER SIX:
# THE SEVEN STEPS - NUMBER 4 PEOPLE

*If you hang out with chickens, you're going to cluck and if you hang out with eagles, you're going to fly."*
~ Steve Maraboli ~

While building resilience is something individuals have to do for themselves, other people can be a great source of support and encouragement.

In this step, we are going to look at how to build great relationships, the role values play in behaviours and the importance of teamwork.

It is said that you should strive to be the person you'd like to meet. If you want to achieve your dreams, you need to develop personally and surround yourself with people of good character who have the skills and attitude that will support you. Who you hang out with is important.

People don't always realise how much they are influenced by others and how easily they can form unhelpful negative habits. As teachers or parents and role models, you can focus on developing positive attitudes and behaviours in young people and help them build supportive networks among their friends, family and others.

Behind great people and their achievements often lies a great team who gives support, shares the vision and has a positive approach to life, based on values and principles. That's why the people you choose are likely to make such a difference to the outcomes you achieve.

How can you develop your people skills and help young people to do the same? This might include:

- How to communicate by asking effective questions and listening empathically.

- How to receive and act on feedback by being open-minded and willing to learn.

- How to find the best solutions where everyone wins, even in difficult situations.

- How to use values to underpin good behaviour.

- How to build a great support team.

- How to be a friend and supporter for others.

## Learning Outcomes

Without a good support team, even well crafted plans might not be as successful as they could be. The Olympic athlete needs their coach, physiotherapist, masseur, doctor, psychologist, nutritionist, and agent. Everyone needs support and students need a diverse range of people who can show them the importance of having the right support group: supporters; teachers, parents, friends and coaches to help inspire them to achieve their dreams.

Here are two ways:

1) Sharing examples of successful people and their teams.

2) Helping students to understand how to build relationships with people who can support and challenge them.

By working through the exercises below, you can help students develop their support team.

## Understanding Your Own and Others' Unconscious Behaviour

Before you can start to build supportive relationships, it is helpful to understand the things that are likely to affect behaviour. At one level behaviours are driven by unconscious patterns, established when people were very young. If and when we become more aware of these drivers, we can adapt and act in a way that is more likely to get the best out of any situation.

Dr William Marston, a psychologist, developed a theory to identify and explain major behavioural styles, which he called DISC, which stands for **D**ominance, **I**nfluence, **S**teadiness, and **C**ompliance. The four styles were derived from two parameters – whether people are more active or passive and whether they see the world as friendly or hostile (see the diagram opposite). This is taken from the Emotions of Normal People, Marston (1928).

To identify your preferred behaviour you can answer the following questions, study the tables on pages 66 and 68 to 71, and then see which best fit how you like to act.

Ask yourself four simple questions:

1. Do you like to be in control and make decisions (**Dominance**), or are you happy to take more of a back seat?

2. Do you like to make friends; network and at least sometimes take centre stage (**Influence**), or are you more comfortable out of the limelight?

3. Do you like to do one job at a time, complete it and are well organised (**Steadiness**), or do you prefer to jump from job to job and you get bored easily?

4. Are you a perfectionist and do you like rules and regulations (**Compliance**), or are you comfortable in making up your own rules and doing what you want?

Answering yes to the first part of any of these questions would give you an indication that your behaviour traits might fit into the area that is highlighted in the brackets. This is a very simple

# Dominance

# Compliance

hostile, unfriendly, antagonistic

active
behaviours

passive
behaviours

friendly, favourable

# Influence

# Steadiness

look at DISC and of course more is needed to arrive at a true profile. If you look at the box below, you will see some of the typical behaviours of people that fall into the various categories and you might recognise more of these traits in yourself. This will provide further guidance in deciding what your behaviour profile might look like.

Do the words in any of the boxes describe how you like to behave?

| D | I | S | C |
|---|---|---|---|
| Dominant | Influential | Steady | Compliant |
| Competitive | Talkative | Dependable | Cautious |
| Forceful | Persuasive | Deliberate | Careful |
| Demanding | Friendly | Persistent | Systematic |
| Direct | Communicative | Good listener | Rule Follower |
| Decisive | Story Teller | Kind | Accurate |
| Seeks Power | Interested | Status Quo | Perfectionist |
| | Networker | Thorough | Logical |

In addition to understanding your preferred behaviour style, you can also identify the sort of environment you like.

Those with **low Dominance** like an environment where they can stand back and take their time over decisions. Words describing their behaviour might include non-assertive, having a low decision need, accommodating, non-demanding and hestitant.

Those with **low Influence** like an environment where they can act on facts and figures and not feelings. Words describing their behaviour might include, reflective, reserved, shy, self-conscious and serious.

Those with **low Steadiness** like an environment where they can juggle lots of different tasks at the same time (they are easily bored). Words describing their behaviour might include restless, fidgeting, active, distracted and mobile.

Finally those with **low Compliance** will like an environment where they are allowed to do things their own way. Words describing their behaviour might include opinionated, persistent, pursuing their own way, strong willed and stubborn.

Once you think you have a good idea about your preferred behaviour style, you can look at the descriptions below, to understand how you might modify your behaviour to help build better relationships with those who like to behave in a different way. This can be a fun exercise to use with students and they can start to identify each other's preferred behaviours and work out how to build stronger relationships, and get the best from each other and their support network.

*Once you think you have a good idea about your preferred behaviour style, you can look at the descriptions below, to understand how you might modify your behaviour to help build better relationships with those who like to behave in a different way.*

## Dominance

| Motivators: | • Achieving results.<br>• Being in control.<br>• Meeting challenges. |
|---|---|
| *Behaviours you might see:* | • Might take over from others.<br>• Often interrupts or doesn't give others time.<br>• Is restless and fidgets.<br>• Shows impatience. May point when talking.<br>• Tells others what to do. |
| *What they want* | • To be in charge and freedom from the control of others.<br>• To escape from detail.<br>• To have clear goals or know the outcome needed.<br>• To try new things.<br>• Variety of tasks.<br>• To be allowed to drive results.<br>• To be able to measure performance.<br>• To negotiate their own actions and outcomes.<br>• To give orders.<br>• To direct others.<br>• To be given independence. |

| Influence | |
|---|---|
| *Motivators:* | • Recognition from others.<br>• Public praise.<br>• Popularity. |
| *Behaviours you might see:* | • Shows enthusiasm.<br>• Is friendly to others.<br>• Moves hands a lot when talking.<br>• Probably tells stories.<br>• Enjoys putting on a performance or being given attention. |
| *What they want* | • To be allowed to speak freely.<br>• To be able to talk with people across boundaries.<br>• To be able to interact with people.<br>• To build relationships.<br>• To be able to work with and through people.<br>• To be recognised for their achievements.<br>• To 'sell' to others.<br>• To be given the opportunity to lead others.<br>• To receive recognition from others and within their organisation. |

| Steadiness | |
|---|---|
| *Motivators:* | • Security. |
| | • Status Quo (no changes). |
| *Behaviours you might see:* | • Likely to be a good listener. |
| | • Relaxed and non-assertive. |
| | • Probably kind and supportive of others. |
| | • Probably resists change. |
| | • Unlikely to show aggression or put up a fight. |
| *What they want* | • Not to be given short or tight deadlines. |
| | • Freedom from pressure. |
| | • A familiar work environment. |
| | • To work within a clear structure. |
| | • To have defined processes. |
| | • To be part of a stable team. |
| | • To have specialised work. |
| | • To have the time to do a thorough job requiring patience. |
| | • To be allowed to follow through and complete tasks. |
| | • To be appreciated with sincerity. |
| | • To have the time to listen. |
| | • To be of service to others. |

## Compliance

| | |
|---|---|
| *Motivators:* | • Working to rules.<br>• Having policies.<br>• Being given full information. |
| *Behaviours you might see:* | • Might make a lot of notes.<br>• Probably very precise and accurate.<br>• Likely to be non expressive or to show feelings.<br>• Probably asks for information and details.<br>• Wants follow up in writing. |
| *What they want* | • Not to work in ambiguity.<br>• To have clear instructions.<br>• To have systems to work with and that work.<br>• To have objectives that are clearly defined.<br>• Not to be subjected to change without good reason.<br>• To have work requiring specialisation.<br>• To work to high standards.<br>• To work within an ordered environment.<br>• To be given all the facts.<br>• To be given information in writing.<br>• Verbal messages to be followed up in writing. |

When you are looking to build effective relationships, it is important to think about how you should adapt your behaviour. The old saying was, 'do unto others as you want to be done unto you'. This isn't enough now or effective.

The saying needs to be 'do unto others as they want to be done to'. As everyone is different, it makes sense to treat people in a way that fits with their behaviour preferences. Yet so many people behave in line with their own preferences when dealing with others and as a result fail to get the best results.

This is a very brief look at the DISC framework. We use DISC and other profiles when working with leaders, individuals, and students to help them become more self-aware and understand the impact they have on themselves and others. It provides a powerful insight for people who want to improve their behaviours or performance.

If you want to know more about William Marston's behaviour theory then you can take a look at his book, 'The Emotions of Normal People'. Marston also introduced the lie detector or polygraph and as a strong advocate of women's rights, he created Wonder Woman for DC comics. His is an interesting story!

> *The saying needs to be 'do unto others as they want to be done to'. As everyone is different, it makes sense to treat people in a way that fits with their behaviour preferences.*

# The Importance of Values in Relationships
# – Creating Conscious Behaviours

Although we are greatly affected by our unconscious behaviour, we are able consciously to manage our actions and words through living to our values. For example, what does the value of respect mean in terms of behaviour? Well, when we show respect (value) to someone else we listen to them and try to understand their point of view (behaviour). We might also demonstrate respect for others by behaviours such as turning up to meetings on time and being prepared for them.

If teams want to work to shared values, then they need to agree these as a group through discussion and then individuals have to commit to using them every day. Think about some of the values that are important in your life as an adult and a teacher. Below are some examples of values and their definitions. Which ones would add value to your students' lives if they were to embrace them?

**Authenticity**: Approaching life by being genuine and yourself.

**Balance**: Where you find a holistic and sustainable way to move forward.

**Commitment**: Willing to put in the time and effort to achieve your goals.

**Compassion**: Understanding and caring about others.

**Courage**: To do what is sometimes difficult or challenging when it is the right choice.

**Creativity**: To develop your ideas, concepts, and personal vision.

**Empathy**: Placing yourself in someone else's shoes for greater understanding.

**Excellence:** Being the best you can be in everything you do in life.

**Fairness:** Treating everyone, as they would want to be treated.

**Faith:** Having a belief in yourself and getting the outcomes you desire.

**Family:** The people with whom you are deeply connected.

**Freedom:** Having the power to make wise choices.

**Friendship:** Understanding that it is important to give as well as to receive from others.

**Generosity:** Realising that sharing with others leads to personal fulfilment.

**Genuineness:** Approaching life through honest and sincere words and actions.

**Happiness:** Is a state where we are open-minded, curious, and positive.

**Harmony:** Working together as one team where our energies align and flow together.

**Health:** A healthy life entails balancing the needs of mind, body, emotion, and spirit.

**Honesty:** Approaching life with genuine intentions, based on truth and goodwill.

**Humour:** Not taking yourself or life too seriously and putting things into perspective.

**Integrity:** Your capacity to do the right thing rather than take the easy option.

**Kindness:** Show care and concern for others through your thoughts and actions.

**Knowledge:** What you know and how you apply it, is what truly makes the difference.

**Loyalty:** Remember your supporters and their contribution to your success.

**Openness:** Being open-minded allows you to consider all possibilities.

**Perseverance:** This means never giving up, even in the face of adversity.

**Respect:** Respect is paying attention to other people's needs and aspirations.

**Responsibility:** Responding consciously rather than reacting unconsciously.

**Security:** Accept your fears and be responsible for your attitude and focus.

**Serenity:** Finding the centre within yourself where you can remain calm.

**Service to others:** Helping others is the right thing to do and it allows you to grow.

**Trust:** This is built by behaving with integrity over a period of time and by delivering on your promises.

Values provide a moral compass that consciously guides you through life, keeping you on your path, and you will often be drawn towards people who hold similar values. When people are led by values such as honesty, trust, and commitment, they can create aligned and powerful teams who are able to achieve great things.

Explore what the above values mean for your students and what behaviour and actions they would be likely to display if they lived to them. Ask them to pick one or two that have real interest for them and to work on them. Follow up with further discussion on what the values are that they would want to see in a supporter.

## Team Work

There is an old used mnemonic which says Team = Together Everyone Achieves More.

Working together as a team and combining each individual's strengths and unique abilities usually results in the whole (team) being stronger than its parts (individuals).

Having a personal support team can add incredible value and assistance and when things are tough, help build and sustain resilience.

Successful teams work with values, but what also makes the difference is having a vision and mission. To create a support team therefore, a young person needs to share their aspirations and help the team understand their vision. Of course, they need to make sure that these are real supporters, because they don't want people who will undermine them.

One other aspect of teamwork is who does what or what role each individual will play within the team. Meredith Belbin, a professor at the Henley Management College, discovered that the most successful teams tended to be those with a mix of different people, i.e. those with a range of different behaviours and skills. In fact, she identified nine distinct team roles and clusters of behaviours, which turned out to be distinctive and useful, with the balance of those required being dependent on the purpose and objectives of the team.

Here are Belbin's nine team roles.

## Plant

Plants are creative, unorthodox and generators of ideas. If an innovative solution to a problem is needed, a Plant is a good person to ask. A good Plant will be bright and freethinking. Plants can tend to ignore incidentals and refrain from getting bogged down in detail. The Plant bears a strong resemblance to the popular caricature of the absent-minded professor/inventor.

## Resource Investigator

The Resource Investigator gives a team a rush of enthusiasm at the start of any project by vigorously pursuing contacts and opportunities. They are focused outside the team, and have a finger firmly on the pulse of the outside world. Where a Plant creates new ideas, a Resource Investigator will quite happily appropriate them from other companies or people. A good Resource Investigator is a creator of possibilities and an excellent networker, but has a tendency to lose momentum towards the end of a project and to forget small details.

## Co-coordinator

A coordinator is a likely candidate for the chairperson of a team, since they have a talent for stepping back to see the big picture. Co-coordinators are confident, stable, and mature and because they recognise abilities in others, they are very good at delegating tasks to the right people for the job. The coordinator clarifies decisions, helping everyone else focus on their tasks.

## Shaper

The Shaper is a task-focused individual who works hard and pursues objectives with vigour and who is driven to achieve objectives. For the Shaper, winning is the name of the game. The Shaper provides the necessary drive to ensure that the team keeps moving and does not lose focus or momentum.

Shapers are people who challenge the team to improve. They are dynamic and usually extroverted people who enjoy stimulating others, questioning norms, and finding the best approaches for solving problems. The Shaper is the one who shakes things up to make sure that all possibilities are considered and that the team does not become complacent. Shapers could risk becoming aggressive and bad-humoured in their attempts to get things done. They often see obstacles as exciting challenges and they tend to have the courage to push on when others feel like quitting.

## Monitor Evaluator
Monitor Evaluators are fair and logical observers and judges of what is going on in the team. Since they are good at detaching themselves from bias, they are often the ones to see all available options with the greatest clarity and impartiality. They take a broad view when problem solving, and by moving slowly and analytically, will almost always come to the right decision.

## Team worker
A Team worker is the oil of the cogs that keeps the machine that is the team, running smoothly. They are good listeners and diplomats, talented at smoothing over conflicts and helping parties understand one another without becoming confrontational. Since the role can be a low-profile one, the beneficial effect of a Team worker can go unnoticed and unappreciated until they are absent, when the team begins to argue, and small but important things cease to happen.

## Implementer
The Implementer takes their colleagues' suggestions and ideas and turns them into positive action. They are efficient and self-disciplined, and can always be relied on to deliver on time. They are motivated by their loyalty to the team or company, which means that they will often take on jobs everyone else, avoids or dislikes.

## Completer Finisher

The Completer Finisher is a perfectionist and will often go the extra mile to make sure everything is 'just right'. The things they deliver have been double-checked and then checked again. Completer Finishers have a strong inward sense of the need for accuracy, and they set high standards.

## Specialist

Specialists are passionate about learning in their own particular field. As a result, they are likely to be fountains of knowledge and they will enjoy imparting this knowledge to others. They also strive to improve and build upon their expertise. If there is anything they do not know the answer to, they will happily go and find out.

## What next?

It would be a good exercise to ask each student what contribution they bring to a team and what roles they need supporters to play, to give them the best support. As a result of looking at DISC, values and Belbin, you and your students should be able to develop strong ideas of what behaviours they need to demonstrate and what they want from a support team.

# Success Stories

**Team GB** at the 2012 London Olympics demonstrated how a support team can bring huge success. The main story starts much earlier in Singapore 2005, when London won the right to host the Games. (The real start was even earlier when the decision to bid for the Games was taken.)

After being awarded the Games the London Organising Committee for the Olympic Games and Paralympic Games was established. It took responsibility for the venues (building many from scratch), transport, getting teams to London and the events, hotel accommodation, education (including school programmes), and many other aspects of the Games.

Led by Sebastian Coe, who inspired so many people to become involved, the Games wouldn't have been delivered without an incredible support team, which included many of the general public, who gave support, bought tickets, and acted as volunteers. It is probably the best UK example of how people pulling together, delivered something incredible. And it didn't stop once the Games started.

Team GB put together a group focused on supporting all the athletes at both the Olympic and Paralympic Games to ensure the best possible results for 'home' competitors. And didn't they deliver?

In addition to the athletes' own programmes and coaches, the English Institute of Sport was engaged and 103 of its practitioners were available to support the 542 athletes at the Olympic Games. This included people accredited to work directly with Team GB, those working at Team GB House or in the Olympic Park, those working close to the Olympic Village, and others working at the Team GB pre-Games preparation camp at Loughborough.

This included, a Head of Performance Services, strength and conditioning coaches, doctors, physiotherapists, psychologists, physiologists, nutritionists, performance analysts, bio-mechanists, performance specialists, administrators, and a press officer. Wow. And this was just one aspect of the comprehensive support provided.

The results were outstanding.

Team GB won 29 Gold, 17 Silver, and 19 Bronze medals at the Olympic Games and finished third in the medals table, punching well above their weight.

At the Paralympic Games, they won 31 Gold, 39 Silver and 38 Bronze medals and finished second in the medal table, behind China.

While it will be difficult for you or any of your students to mobilise anywhere near this level of support, it is clear that everyone has a choice to make. Will you be the one who seeks out support and also inspires others through giving support, or not? Start now and use your personal influence to connect with other people, engage their support and be part of their support team and encourage your students to do the same.

**Apollo 13** - many people will be familiar with the story of Apollo 13, thanks to the 1995 Ron Howard movie of the same name. This revolves around a mission to the moon by NASA that went badly wrong. Unfortunately, there was an explosion on the space capsule.

Suddenly the radio link with the crew crackled to life. "Okay Houston, we've had a problem here." The explosion had caused a malfunction in the control system, which was needed to keep the spaceship pointing in the right direction and there was also liquid oxygen spilling out from the damaged service module.

The flight director, Kranz was told, "Flight, I have got a feeling we've lost two fuel cells. I hate to put it that way, but I don't know why we've lost them."

It was about 45 minutes after the explosion, and the backroom team estimated that at the oxygen supply's current rate of decay, they would lose the last fuel cell in less than 2 hours. "That's the end right there," said one of the technicians.

Kranz said. "I want you to get some guys figuring out the minimum power to sustain life and a way to get them home safely."

It doesn't sound like a —big task. The lunar module had big, charged batteries, and was full of oxygen tanks, which were all designed to last the duration of Apollo 13's lunar excursion (some 33 hours on the surface). So it should have been a simple matter of flipping a few switches, to turn on the power and getting the life-support system running, right?

Unfortunately, spaceships don't work like that. They have complicated, interdependent, systems that have to be turned on in just the right sequence as dictated by lengthy checklists. Miss a step and you can do irreparable damage. The problem was that the main capsule, Odyssey, was now irreparable and they had to use the support capsule as a lifeboat to get the astronauts home.

Nobody had ever planned for this situation, but a dedicated team began working out a set of ad-hoc procedures. These were step by step, switch by switch instructions for the astronauts, which would coax enough power, through the maze of circuits, for a return journey home. Working from wiring and equipment diagrams of the lunar module, it took them just 30 minutes to finish the list of instructions to begin to power up the life-support systems in lifeboat mode; although it was anticipated, it would take several hours.

With only about 15 minutes of oxygen left in the main spacecraft, they completed their task and avoided disaster.

The stakes in this story were really high; if mission control had failed, then the astronauts would not have survived. Yet the message is clear, in life all of us need help and support, so having a great team around us is really important and in some cases can mean the difference between life and death.

## Thought Momentum

As a teacher, you can share motivational stories about people who have had amazing lives. Choosing roles models with positive messages can inspire young people to start their own journey of discovery and gives them the encouragement to overcome any obstacles.

The best people to be in your team, are those that will support you and add the most value. For young people, their team will mostly consist of family, teachers, mentors and friends, who are dedicated to helping them, achieve their best. They all need to play a role in building the essential life skills, attitudes, and values that will carry them into adulthood.

Conversely, if you surround yourself with the wrong people, then you are likely to be dragged down to their level. We can't always choose our teachers and parents and perhaps that isn't fair, but we can help young people determine what good team players look like and how they are able to make wise choices.

## Taking the Next Step

Young people are often told by adults who they should or shouldn't hang out with, but people don't often discuss what constitutes a good role model or supporter. Teachers can play their part in sharing the reasons why it is important for students to surround themselves with the right people, and explain what a good supporter can do for them.

For example, a supporter could:

- Listen to them and understand their hopes and dreams.
- Be their conscience when they have committed to take action.
- Encourage and praise them.

- Ask effective questions that help them to think of good ideas and solutions.

- Give feedback on their progress.

- Support them in learning new skills and knowledge.

  The role of a supporter and coach is to help the young person become more self-aware and responsible for the choices they make. The first step to discovering the importance of having a support team is to have a discussion on its benefits. Ask them: Why might it be important to have a support team?

  Some of the answers you can expect during a class discussion might include:

- They may give time, energy, and practical support when it is needed.

- They may help with any difficulties in school, with a subject, another person, or at home.

- They may give advice on different courses of action.

- They may listen to concerns or plans.

- They may help with the learning of new skills or developing a more positive can-do attitude.

- They may share their own experiences to increase understanding and improve decision- making.

You can take the discussion further and include specific examples of support teams. It's a great opportunity for them to do the following:

- Pinpoint whom they need and can appreciate in their lives. People such as friends, neighbours, parents, grandparents, coaches, and teachers may be on this list.

- Think about those people who are already supporting them and how they can make the most of this. This list will most likely include some of the same people as are listed in the bullet point above.

Young people often employ support teams when following their hobbies and interests. The young ballerina is inspired by the teacher who shows them how to excel and improve; the soccer player responds to the coach who reminds them of their strengths and makes suggestions on how to improve; and a child who wants to be able to sing better sees the value in the advice their music teacher gives them.

Everywhere we look in this world, we see support teams, making things more cohesive and people happier. Teachers can show students how to create a network of people that want them to succeed, celebrate their success or encourage them when they are down or things are not going as well as they would like.

When choosing a supporter it helps to define their characteristics. Some of these are listed above in this chapter in *The Values Network*. As a reminder, these values may include:

*Authenticity, balance, commitment, compassion, courage, creativity, empathy, excellence, fairness, freedom, friendship, generosity, happiness, honesty, humour, integrity, kindness, knowledge, loyalty, openness, perseverance, respect for others, responsibility, and trust.*

Take some time with your students, ask which values are important to them, and encourage them to give examples of these in action. It's also helpful for you as a teacher, to share the values that are important to you. For example, if you value the quality of commitment you can share stories around it and any associated behaviours.

Another exercise you can use is to have your class choose their top three values.

Start by asking each student to choose three values from the list that are important to them. You can do this by writing them on a whiteboard and asking every class member to vote for their choice by putting three marks or ticks against their choice or through a show of hands. The values with the most votes get to be chosen as the 'class values'.

After the top three values are identified, ask the students to discuss how they can turn these values into behaviours, giving specific examples of what they can do to demonstrate that they are using them every day.

An example is if trust is one of the chosen values, they can talk about delivering on their promises. If they say they will do something, then they should follow through on their commitment. Once the action has been completed and the commitment honoured, trust will grow. Each student needs to be personally responsible for acting out the agreed behaviours. It's not always easy to have integrity, but it can start with simple lessons like these and develop into a set of values, which will underpin great relationships and a strong support team.

From there, you can address how students feel about people who don't share the same values as them. Ask them the following questions and discuss their answers:

- How do you feel when someone behaves differently to your personal values? Do you judge them or try to understand their point of view? Sometimes it's okay to be different and you can work with them even if you don't always agree.

- How do you deal with people who don't have the same values as you? Do you say something, walk away, or try to lead by example?

The way people behave greatly affects relationships. That's why there is no magic formula to human relationships and interaction, only guidelines that have been proven to be effective. Talk with the class about positive ways to look at big differences. Focus on points such as:

- Gaining a higher level of awareness.
- Showing tolerance.
- Having and developing understanding.
- Being patient.
- Being able to respond to any situation positively rather than act through a lack of understanding and awareness.

By this time, your students are going to have a strong grasp of the fundamentals of support teams and how they can be a motivator and provide a competitive advantage. That is when you can leave them with one last impactful question. Ask them: What is one thing you can do today to improve a relationship or find a support team member?

Step four for building resilience – people. Surround yourself with amazing and inspiring people!

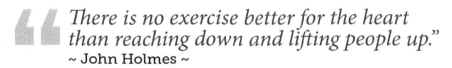

*There is no exercise better for the heart than reaching down and lifting people up."*
~ John Holmes ~

# CHAPTER SEVEN:
# THE SEVEN STEPS – NUMBER 5 PLANNING

*Productivity is never an accident. It is always the result of a commitment to excellence, intelligent planning, and focused effort."*
~ Paul J. Meyer ~

It's all in the planning. Have you heard that before? Chances are you have and it's absolutely true. Planning is both important and necessary. If you want favourable odds for success, you can't just hope for the best. You need to make things happen. As a teacher, you can show your students how to create plans that work for them and get them to where they want to be in life!

In this chapter, we will share the way to transform a dream into practical plans and use the grow model as a way of having coaching conversations to achieve goals.

## Three levels of goal setting

The gift of the teacher, manager, or coach is to help their students, employees or coachees to gain goal clarity. So many people do not know what they really want, not just on simple issues but in life in general. The first question to ask is, "What do you want to achieve?" However, it is helpful to take a step back, in order to understand that goals can be set at different levels.

### Visionary goals (outcomes)

At the highest level, we look at visionary or dream goals. For example, when John F Kennedy first had the vision to send astronauts to the moon, it seemed impossible and would stretch the scientists' knowledge, technology and capability to the limits. Yet it galvanised people towards achieving a big goal.

To achieve a visionary goal, an individual needs to have the motivation to complete it and this may require large amounts of energy, commitment and sacrifice. It is only when individuals have a genuine mission and passion to succeed, that they embark on such tough challenges.

People have limited control over the achievement of visionary goals, as any outcome will always be uncertain.

A further good example is the ambitions of Olympic athletes. For some, their dream goal may be to stand on the top of the podium with a gold medal around their neck, and for others it may be to go to the Olympics. However, the only control they have is over what they do and they cannot control the performance of others, so whether they achieve the outcome or not, is only partly down to them.

Your role as a teacher is to help students to create a powerful vision, with as much detail as possible (what it feels, sound and looks like), which will drive them forward.

**Performance goals (outputs)**
The second tier of goal setting is performance goals, which we sometimes refer to as objectives.

The main aim of a visionary goal is to be aspirational, and to inspire and motivate, whereas, a performance goal is designed to be practical. These are goals that are within the performer's control. So if a student wants to go to college or university (dream goal), they need to have personal performance goals like working towards achieving certain grades in their examinations.

In the case of an Olympian, this will be about delivering their personal best on the day, to reach the Olympics or to win that medal in the final. If they do this and someone performs better than they do, then they have still achieved the best performance possible.

**Process goals (inputs)**
The third tier of goal setting is process goals (inputs).

These are the 'how to' of achieving the performance and dream goals. One example is the learning and revision that needs to be completed, if students are to achieve the grades they want and the university place that may follow.

To help you to be clear about performance and process goals, they are often referred to as SMART goals. Specific, Measurable, Ambitious, Relevant and Timed.

**Specific** – Is the goal clear and precise and has positive focus?

**Measurable** – Can the goal be measured so you can track progress and know when you have been successful?

**Ambitious** – Is the goal challenging enough to make it worthwhile and achievable?

**Relevant** – Does the goal align to and support the vision you have?

**Timed** – Is the goal set in a timeframe, which will encourage you to take action?

**Important criteria for goal setting**

- Goals need to be framed positively. What you do want rather than what you don't want. I want to succeed rather than I don't want to fail.

- Visionary goals need to be aligned with performance goals. For example, winning a gold medal at the Olympics (vision) needs to be aligned with achieving a time that puts you in with a chance (for example running below 10 seconds for the 100 metres).

- It is helpful for teachers (or any coach), to agree with their students (or coachees) what can be called stepped or variable performance goals. You do this by helping them to set out minimum and maximum levels of goal achievement. Some people find it motivational to have a minimum level of achievement, which is acceptable and achievable, so that every performance should produce a positive result.

- Goals should always be reviewed if they are to continue to be motivational.

- Performance goals must be within the performer's control (at least a significant part of it).

**A story to illustrate the importance of understanding goals: Lynn Davies CBE**
Lynn was born on the 20th May 1942 and is a Welsh former track and field athlete who specialised in the long jump.

In 1964, he won the Olympic Gold medal for the long jump in Tokyo (earning himself the nickname "Lynn the Leap") with a jump of 8.07 meters.

In the summer of 1968, he was in the best shape of his life and had achieved Olympic winning scores in some events, as he approached the Mexico Olympic Games.

His dream (vision) was to retain his title and win gold once again. This was also eminently achievable and realistic. However, in the first legal jump of the games, the American long jumper Bob Beamon broke the world record with a jump of 8.90 meters (55 centimetres or approximately 2 feet beyond the then current record).

Lynn Davies is quoted as saying to Beamon, "You have destroyed this event," and in sports jargon, a new adjective – Beamonesque – came into use to describe spectacular feats. Lynn accepted that his dream goal of winning had gone and he ended up only being placed 9th in the event.

Years later, Lynn was introduced to the concept of the three levels of goal setting and he said that although he wouldn't have won gold in Mexico, if he had only focused on and achieved his personal best performance, and not given up, he would have won the silver medal. This also ties in with having the right mindset, which we explore in a later chapter.

While it is important to have a vision or dream goal, you cannot always control the outcome of this. You must focus on your performance and process goals, which you can control, if you want to be the best you can be.

*Once you are clear about your goals, planning then becomes the important element in achieving them. An effective plan allows you to focus your thoughts, time and energy on the actions, which will enable you to deliver the outcomes you want. The saying, 'if you fail to plan then you plan to fail', is true and without a plan your actions will not be congruent with what you want to achieve.*

## Learning Outcomes

Thinking about planning and implementing plans, are two different things. Both are necessary, and the first step is to create the plan on which you can act to deliver the results you want. As you go through this chapter, you will find ideas that will work for you and your students. You can begin instilling the importance of planning and begin showing how to put a successful plan together.

Two lessons that you will take away from this chapter are:

1) A better understanding of successful people and how they plan for their success. They set goals, take steps that are within their control, and develop a toolbox of skills that help them in the process.

Some of the skills that people develop as part of their personal toolbox include:

- Setting smart goals.

- Managing their time effectively.

- Prioritising the important things to do.

- Sharing their goals with those who will help to deliver them.

- Building the confidence to try new things and committing to action.

2) A better understanding of the planning process. As a teacher, you can show your students, by your example, how you have put plans into action and been successful.

Effective planning often starts with having a vision or a big goal and understanding what you are prepared to do to achieve it. If it is something you really want, then the next step is to break this down into smaller pieces that are easy to tackle. These are smaller goals and are sometimes known as milestones. It is this process, which can turn a concept or dream into a tangible result.

It also helps to link your vision and goals with your passion and positive emotions, as these will give you the energy and drive to pursue them. Why is that? When you visualise success as we have discussed in previous chapters, using all your senses, you create a powerful mindset that can assist you in achieving the outcomes you want. For example if you were to plan an outstanding lesson:

- You can visualise yourself walking into your lesson, seeing the children settling down and listening to you intently.

You can see them working and learning collaboratively, producing good work and making progress.

- You can imagine hearing them asking each other thought-provoking questions and listening to each other with respect. You can hear your voice as you confidently share ideas and knowledge with your students. You get the sense of the excitement amongst your students, as they enjoy your lesson and you feel a sense of pride in your positive and professional approach.

- You feel you can smell and taste success.

Using your visualisation and senses in this way, can make any plan seem real and if you play a successful lesson out in your mind, it will give you the confidence to try new things.

Now we will look at a model you can use for planning.

## G.R.O.W.

G.R.O.W. is a mnemonic that stands for Goal, Reality, Options and Will. It is used by many performance coaches to help people plan how they will achieve their goals. Quite simply it is like a satellite navigation system that many people have in their cars. The first step is knowing where you want to go (Goal), next the GPS or global positioning system knows where you are now (Reality), and from that information it suggests routes (Options) for you and finally you agree the route you will take (Will).

At the end of this chapter, there are some great questions you can ask yourself and your students to effectively identify each step of the plan using this model, but before that, let's look at each of the steps in turn:

**G:** The *G* represents your Goal. The first step to success is defining a goal that you want to achieve. This could also be expressed as an issue you want to resolve. Goals are linked to the future and they take you to the place where you would like to be. As a teacher, your students may wish to make progress in areas such as sports, hobbies and interests, academic subjects, home life, and relationships.

We have already discussed the SMART framework for goals and we really encourage you to follow this.

A major mistake many people make is to have a lack of clarity about their goal. It is not enough to say my goal is to be successful. It helps to know what your success looks like or feels like, so zhat you will know when you have achieved it.

It is helpful to be able to measure success by understanding numbers, for example, how much, how many and how often? It's good if your goals are stretching, because if they are too easy they probably aren't worthwhile. If you do set yourself a big goal, you can break it down and set some milestones along the way to motivate you and keep you on track. As we have already said you must set clear time frames, because having deadlines can help prioritise your time and energy. Finally, make sure you have a strong interest and passion for your goals, as this will give you the motivation to keep going even when times are tough.

**R:** The *R* represents Reality. The second step is to determine where you are now in relation to where you want to be in the future. This will help you understand some of the issues surrounding your goal. It will give you the opportunity to dig down and examine all the facts and problems that might stop you moving forward. It is useful to review what is happening now, what you have tried already and what results you have achieved so far. We can also get others people's perspective on some of the issues to help gain greater clarity.

Using the analogy of the satellite navigation system, if you don't know your starting point, you are unlikely to be able to plot the best route to get to the destination you want.

<u>O:</u> The O represents Options. The options are the ideas and methods to help us move towards our goal. This is where creative thinking is allowed and encouraged. There is an old saying that there is more than one right answer. So we ask students to generate lots of ideas, then choose the ones for which they have most interest and that will ensure they pursue their goal. If your students get stuck, you can ask questions such as "What else?" or "What if?" (hypothetical questions) to encourage them to go beyond any possible limited thinking.

This might include "what if you could do anything, had more time, had all the money you needed, what would you do?"

To give an example of generating options, perhaps you can think about planning an outstanding lesson. What ideas or options might you have: you could research new ways of presenting your content, you could use multimedia, you could use new exercises or games to demonstrate points, you could organise individual or group work and you could work with other departments and have joint lessons or themed projects.

Once you have pulled out lots of ideas, then chose the ones that most suit you, your lesson and your students, not forgetting that sometimes it's good to try something new.

It is often helpful to write down your options and once you are confident you have exhausted your thinking, you can work through each idea in turn and see whether it is something, you want to pursue. Write a score of between 1 and 10 against each option, where ten means you have a real interest and strong motivation in pursuing this option, and one you have no interest at all.

**W:** The *W* represents what you **Will** do to achieve your goal. This is the action step, where you take your options and put them into action. You cannot achieve your goals by thinking alone, because without action nothing happens. It's at this stage that your options/ideas need to be reviewed, to ensure that they are aligned to your goals.

Once you have chosen the options that are of most interest to you (those scoring 10 or close to it), then record what it is that you will actually do to move it forward.

Ask yourself what the first step will be and when you will take it. This may be as simple as having a conversation with someone to gain support, pulling a team together or carrying out a very specific task, for example writing something. Whatever it is, you need to write down exactly what you will do.

Then you will need to decide when you will take this first action. This should be more than just saying I will do it by a certain date, because often, that time just comes and goes without anything happening. It is much better to be specific in your timing, for example I will do it on Tuesday at 3pm and write it in your diary. In this way you will be committing yourself.

The last thing to complete in the Will section of GROW is to check your level of commitment to take action. Ask yourself the following question, on a scale of 1 to 10, how committed are you to taking the first step? If the answer is less than ten, there is some sort of blockage. There is normally one of three things that stop people taking action. Firstly, the person is not clear about their goal or it's not enough of a priority for them (head/thought). Secondly, they might not have the confidence or courage to start (heart/feeling).

Thirdly, they might not have the get up and go or right intent (guts/will). If this happens, then as a teacher you can ask what is stopping them, and what it will take to get them moving.

## Success Stories

Many of us will agree that when somebody wants something, they can achieve it if they set their minds to it. There's an old story you may have heard, which exemplifies the spirit of success.

There once was a young man who desired to improve his life in a meaningful and significant way. He went to Socrates, the great philosopher, and asked him about the secrets of achieving success. He received an invitation to meet Socrates down by the river the next morning.

Naturally, the young man was excited by the opportunity of talking with the man who many revered and feared. He went to the river the next morning and much to his surprise, Socrates started walking into the river itself. Not sure what to do, the young man followed, wondering what lesson needed to be taught in the river.

Eventually the water was up to their necks and in a shocking and unexpected move, Socrates dunked the young man under the water. He struggled, obviously not happy about such a surprise, and tried to move his head out of the water. Eventually his face started to turn blue and then Socrates let him up.

The young man was gasping and breathing in the air as fast as he could. He was desperate to collect his wits and restore his oxygen levels.

Socrates asked, "What did you want the most when you were under water?"

"Air," the young man replied.

Socrates smiled, looking into the curious young man's eyes. "That's the secret to success. When you want success as badly as you wanted the air just a minute ago, then you will get it. There is no other secret."

Whether you have heard that story or another one like it, too many people now seem to look for fast routes to success, hoping things will just happen for them.

Most people don't have the opportunity to ask a modern day Socrates how to go about achieving success. They learn from their own experiences and other inspiring stories of successful people. One ingredient that is sure to come up is the ability to put together a well thought out plan and stick to it. When you have a real desire to achieve something, it energises your thoughts and actions. As Nike would say – Just do it!

If you can help your students to understand this (without of course having to actually experience the sensation of drowning), then they will be more likely to plan effectively and achieve the things they set out to do.

**Helen Keller** is someone who provides another great example and you may have heard about her or read her many inspirational quotes. There are two things we inevitably remember about her: she could not see or hear. It was the result of contracting an unknown illness (possibly Scarlet Fever) at nineteen months of age, which changed her life forever.

Not surprisingly, as Helen got older she was filled with anger and frustration about her physical limitations. She lashed out and her parents felt so guilty about her plight that they let her do what she wanted. She did take full advantage too, but despite this, she also showed that she had talent and learned over sixty customised hand gestures, which helped her communicate with her parents.

Then the day of reckoning came for Helen. At the age of seven, she was introduced to someone who would hold her to account and who refused to accept that being unable to see or hear, was an excuse for poor behaviour. Anne Sullivan, a private tutor, was recommended by Alexander Graham Bell and was hired to work with Helen. She was just twenty years old.

There was a clash of wills when Helen first encountered her strict new teacher, but Anne didn't give up. She continued to hold Helen accountable for what she did. Helen started to change and saw that the things in her life that she used to term as unfair were actually tools that she could use, to teach others about what it was like to be deaf and blind.

With the help of her mentor and now friend, Helen began setting goals, making plans and taking specific steps to achieve them. Was it easy? No! However, as she conquered goal after goal, she found herself in the position of getting to meet some of the most prominent people in the world, including kings, queens, leaders, and other famous personalities.

Helen also continued to develop her own language, as well as learning Greek, French, and Latin. Nobody would have thought it possible and she demonstrated what a difference the right mentor makes, for putting things into perspective. Without Anne, she may never have gone on to do these amazing things.

Some of the things that Helen did, many would not have thought possible, and they included horse riding, teaching, writing books, and raising public awareness about the true potential of people with disabilities. This once defiant and angry child had turned into a great advocate and an example of what determination, hard work, and following through on your plans can bring.

It is interesting that Helen didn't start with a grand vision, but started out with small steps, built her confidence, increased her skills, and realised that her only limits were in her mind. She was in charge of her own destiny.

For many others who achieve success, it seems to come later in life or follows some tragic event or unexpected change, which forces them to take action. That is what happened to author **Anthony Burgess**.

At the age of forty, Anthony learned he had brain cancer and would be dead within a year. He realised he had a decision to make. Would he just accept his fate and wait to die? Or, would he make the most of his last year and do something that he knew he was capable of – writing? He chose to write.

Anthony had never focused much effort on being a novelist before his diagnosis, but he saw that by pursuing it in the last year of his life was a way to achieve two goals:

- Fulfil something he'd always wanted to do.

- Leave a source of financial security for his family through possible royalties.

With these two clear goals in mind and a plan to put into effect, Anthony began writing. He sat down and took action by putting a piece of paper into the typewriter (yes, this was pre-computer days), and then he let his ideas pour out. He worked passionately and diligently because he found that he truly enjoyed writing. It wasn't always easy, writer's block came as it does for many, but he kept going, never surrendering to negative thoughts like *does this really matter?* It did matter a great deal to him.

With *five complete manuscripts,* Anthony reached the one-year mark, which was the time he was supposed to die because of his brain cancer. Only he didn't die. He felt more alive than ever and better than he had in a long while. His cancer had gone into remission and he went on to write over seventy novels, including classics like *A Clockwork Orange.*

Isn't it amazing to think that Anthony may have never attempted what he was truly destined to do, without the serious push that came from being diagnosed with cancer and being told the odds were not good?

His story is a great lesson to stop putting off your dreams and goals, to plan and to take action. You don't have to wait for bad news, as there is no better day than today, to put a plan in place and to make a start.

## Thought Momentum

There is so much to think about and consider when it comes to planning. For many of us life just gets in the way. We are so busy and with so many distractions hitting us from so many sources (the internet, gadgets, phones, e-mails, work, etc.), it sometimes makes your head spin.

Once you are clear about what it is you want to achieve, you have to plan to achieve it.

*Without a plan any goal is just a dream.*

So stop putting off what you want to achieve and start to make a plan, one step at a time. If you do this, then things will become easier and two things take place:

1)  You can begin enjoying a more purposeful and fulfilled life. Imagine having your other goals, aside from

excellence in teaching, becoming a part of your reality. It would certainly be motivational and invigorating.

2) You can also teach others about how to start planning to achieve their goals and taking steps to achieve them.

Take a moment and think about what you have achieved in your life and how it made you feel. Tap into those experiences and search for examples to share with your students, to show them how you and others plan and successfully achieve goals. They'll appreciate what you share and it will remind you of your many successes.

## Taking the Next Step

There are exciting and specific action steps that teachers can take with students, to help them learn how to put a great plan into place and actually follow through with it. They will enjoy remembering the feeling of achievement when they worked on a plan and saw it through to the end, learning and growing in meeting their challenges.

### Determine why planning is important

Once you explain to your students the importance of planning, they will be more likely to plan for themselves.

Take some time to talk with your students and get them to see the value in:

*"Stop putting off what you want to achieve and start to make a plan, one step at a time."*

- Planning to achieve something, for example, if you want to get a good mark in that science test, you need to study the material. Otherwise, you cannot expect to do well. You also need to pay attention in class and make efforts to absorb what the teacher is saying.

- Recognise what you can and can't control in relation to your goal. For example, if your plan is to mow five lawns every weekend so you can have enough money to purchase that video game you like, what happens if it rains nearly every weekend? Well you can't control the weather so how do you get around obstacles? Do you mow the lawns in the week or find another way of making money?

- What is your response to situations like this that you cannot control? This is an important issue, as it addresses the need to maintain a positive attitude when things don't go the way you want. Never giving up on your goals, is linked directly to resilience and having a successful mindset.

## Make time to G.R.O.W.

As a teacher, helping them to understand and demonstrate the G.R.O.W. model, by walking them through an example, will be a great help. It is a skill that will benefit them in the classroom and throughout their lives.

## G.R.O.W. questions

Below are some questions you can use to help. Goal, Reality, and Option are all awareness raising questions and the Will questions encourage them to take personal responsibility for action.

## G is for GOAL:

This is where you'll determine what you really want to achieve. Have a discussion based around the following questions and make sure your students write down everything that comes into their minds:

- What are some things that you would like to achieve? Ask them to list out anything that comes into their heads. If some get stuck, then share your ideas or ask your class to share theirs.

- From the things they have listed, ask them to choose one that they would most like to achieve (one usually sticks out more than the others do). What will success look like for them? Ask them to think about how it will make them feel and what others will think or say.

- How much personal control do you have in achieving your goal? It is important to determine how much a student can do, compared to how much they have to rely on the support of others.

- How long will it take to achieve your goal? Very few meaningful goals can be achieved overnight or within a few days. You want students to focus on goals that build resilience and determination for the long term. Ask them to write down when they will achieve their goal and if it is a big goal, it may be helpful to break this down into smaller milestones, each with their own time frame.

## R is for REALITY:

This is where you evaluate your present situation in relation to the goal you are planning to achieve. Consider things like:

- What is happening now in relation to this goal? What is the current situation?

- Who else is currently involved? This might be parents, teachers, friends, coaches, or others who are physically helping (or hindering) your plan.

- Who else might be involved indirectly in you achieving your goal?

- What steps have you already taken to achieve this goal? This might be things such as

  o Taking lessons.
  o Asking others.
  o Carrying out research.
  o Other specific things you have tried.
  o Ideas you have or thoughts that are holding you back.

- Determine what the results of your efforts to date have been for your goal. What have you learned so far and how have you used this to plan your next action?

- Did you have success? If you did, why? It may have been because you worked hard for it. Or, did you fall short of what you wanted? If so what did you do next? The point is to emphasise that you don't surrender, you keep trying and you don't assume that it will always be easy because you had a minor victory.

## O is for OPTION:

In order to achieve a goal you need to have ideas or options. Often when you ask students to give some ideas, they may come up with one or two and the role of the coach is to pull more out. When they have lots of ideas, they can make a choice as to which one suits their needs best.

Try this exercise with your students:

- Have your students take some time to list *five* things they can do to help them achieve their goal.

- Rate each idea on a scale of 1 – 10, ten being the most desirable and one being the least desirable (in their opinion).

The highest ranking options are the ones that the students should focus on first, as they are the ones where they have the most interest. Explain that the other options may be good too, but can be used as a backup if things change and the first options are no longer possible.

## W is for WILL:

It's often been said that where there's a will, there's a way. The Will section of the grow model is all about making choices and taking action. Here are some questions that will help:

- What are you going to commit to doing to achieve your goal? When something is important, you tend to put less important events in your life to one side. For example, the karate student working towards their black belt will put in extra time practising instead of watching a movie.

- To what extent do the actions you choose, align with your plan? Many people fall victim to 'busy work' instead of the work that is truly productive. If you want to be able to score more soccer goals, are you better off practising getting the ball in the net, or reading about how others have learned to score more goals? There are times when physically taking action is the right thing to do. It's learning from practical experience.

- How do you measure success? Understanding what your 'success looks like', is important to help you be clear about your goals. It enables you to:
  o See where you still have to go.
  o See how far you've come.
  o Keep driving to cross the finish line.

- What is the first step you are going to take to achieve your goal? This is where a person's will, interacts with their desire to act. It's that moment when the person who is committed to gaining a healthier lifestyle, actually gets out of bed a little earlier to walk to work or school, instead of hitting the snooze button on the alarm clock. It's often the point where you may realise that despite your ambition, taking action isn't always easy. However, once taking action becomes your habit, then achieving your goals becomes easier each day.

- What obstacles and challenges will get in the way and how will you overcome them? This is where many people stop short. They may think I can't go back to college because I'm not good enough, or I may be short of money. Is that truly a reason not to pursue higher education, if that's your dream? Absolutely not! It's a fear mechanism; something designed to protect you from possible failure. To understand that these emotions may come in to play when you're pursuing a goal is important. As a teacher, you can let your students know that it is okay to hesitate or feel afraid, but not to give up.

- Who do you tell? Not all goals need to be shared. Some are personal in nature. However, sharing your goals with others can provide some great benefits, including:
    - Building a support team.
    - Supporters helping you to be accountable for actions and results.
    - Letting others know what's important to you.
    - Finding people to help with specific knowledge or insight.

When you share your plan it's good to evaluate what help you will need and ask your supporters what they can offer.

Now that you've made the commitment, it's time to rate on that scale of 1 – 10 how willing you are to take the action. If you find that you have a low score, it is time to start over! You've likely chosen a goal that doesn't really fit with your passion or your desire to succeed.

When done with enthusiasm and an open mind, the two exercises listed above, can really help a student go from feeling disengaged to feeling fully committed about their future success. That is a real game changer.

Step five to resilience is planning – it is the 'what' and 'how' added to the 'why' (purpose) that makes the difference.

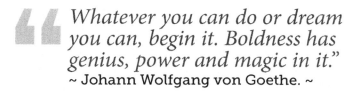

*Whatever you can do or dream you can, begin it. Boldness has genius, power and magic in it."*
~ Johann Wolfgang von Goethe. ~

# CHAPTER EIGHT: THE SEVEN STEPS – NUMBER 6 POSITIVE MINDSET

> *" Whether you think you can or think you can't, you are right."*
> ~ Henry Ford ~

Make it your mantra to be positive in life, because it makes all the difference and defines what you are likely to achieve each and every day. Mentally, you can be your own worst enemy or your best cheerleader. The choice is yours and your mindset is everything.

When it comes to mindset, you have three choices: Negative, Neutral, and Positive. A neutral or negative mindset either leads to stagnation and apathy, or creates thinking, which can result in a can't do attitude and even depression. However, if you adopt a positive mindset, you tend to look at problems as opportunities and make the best out of any situation.

In life you do have control over the way you think (attitude) and your focus. Your thoughts can either energise or drain you. You really do have a choice over which thoughts you want to embrace, so why not choose positive ones. Don't settle for anything less because you deserve more.

People are naturally drawn to others who think positively and it's easily identified in people through:

- Posture (usually head up, back straight, looking confident).

- Mannerisms (smiling, greeting and handshake).

- Words (I will, rather than I will just try or I am taking action, rather than just talking about it).

- Attitude (I believe in myself, I can do it, I will take a risk, I will overcome any obstacles, rather than I can't, it's too scary and I can't overcome that).

It's difficult to fake a positive mindset. Take a moment to reflect on the positive people that you are drawn to most. It feels good to be around someone that believes in possibilities and opportunities and 'everything is going to be alright'. In fact, it's contagious.

That is why positive teachers are more inspirational and have a bigger impact on students. They naturally inspire others to see their strengths and help them to believe in themselves. They help them to know they can do great things, regardless of their environment or situation. It's within a positive culture that seeds can be planted for achievement and success. It is the glue that holds all of the things together, which you've been reading about in this book.

## Learning Outcomes

Some people have a positive attitude every day, and if you are one of them, you are in the right position to be a role model and teach this to your students. You may feel that teaching and demonstrating a positive mindset is challenging, given the amount of work you have to do and the changes in the profession. It may involve changing the way you think, the words you use and even the way you stand. Yet if you can develop this attribute more in yourself, you can really help build it in your students.

An example of a positive mindset is demonstrated by a student who doesn't get the job that they wanted, or who doesn't get picked for the school team but doesn't stop looking or trying. They don't think of themselves or the situation as hopeless. They learn from their experience, plan for the next interview or team try out and keep going until they succeed. Sometimes of course, things don't go to plan, but holding a positive mindset, enables you to bounce back quickly, instead of being trapped in a cycle of negative thinking.

Everyone can learn to:

- Link the benefits of having a positive mental attitude with successful behaviour. Think of how the leaders of organisations, managers, captains of sports teams and successful head teachers, help to inspire their people. When they take the stage, they deliver optimism and positive energy and they always focus on possibilities, and what is achievable. That's where true leaders add real value.

- Identify thinking skills and behaviours associated with a positive mental attitude. Positive thoughts can be used as triggers, to create effective habits and hold off negative feelings and thoughts.

- Understand strategies that help build and maintain a positive mindset.

  The words *positive mindset* are linked with Meta-Cognition or thinking about thinking. Young people who are aware of the way they think, can (with some self-discipline), choose to focus on positive thoughts and allow negative ones to disappear. Teachers can help their students recognise their thinking patterns, for example asking about their most often recurring thoughts in difficult situations. Once they have identified these they can choose to disregard the negative ones, and focus on thoughts that are more positive and empowering. This in turn, will lead to better outcomes.

  Some schools, such as Leighton Park and Marlborough College (among others), have taken steps to help students better focus on the positive outcomes they seek, through allowing them to spend some quiet time. For a short period every day, or for longer periods weekly, they ask their students to spend time thinking, providing the opportunity and room to consider options, think about their strategies, and to prepare themselves effectively for what they want to achieve.

## Win/Lose versus Win/Learn

We have already covered this in Step 1 Place, yet it is such a strong and powerful idea that it is worth reinforcing. The paradigm that many people follow is to think that if they don't win, they lose. This convention can be challenged, by considering if you learn something from an experience, irrespective of the outcome, then you are a winner and not a loser. The only way you can win/lose is if you are not willing to learn and grow from what you do. In life no matter what the circumstances and how difficult they may be, there is always an opportunity to use an experience positively. It may be that you learn:

- You have a lot more grit than you ever thought – that you can persevere against difficult circumstances; that you are a resilient person who understands that adversity is not associated with negativity or failure, but with growth.

- You can do things that you never thought possible. For example, look at the number of people who now run marathons. Many of them didn't think they had the physical capability before they started. Making it through their first marathon without collapsing would be a great reward, and even if they came last, it is still an achievement and it gives them great confidence to attempt other life goals.

- You know what not to do, which is exactly what Thomas Edison meant when he said, *"If I find 10,000 ways something won't work, I haven't failed. I am not discouraged, because every wrong attempt discarded is often a step forward."*

The 10,001 attempt worked of course, when he switched on his light bulb, and as they say, 'The rest is history'.

Thomas Edison also said, *"Many of life's failures are experienced by people who did not realise how close they were to success when they gave up."* In the film Meet the Robinson's, the family says, *"In failure you learn; in success, not so much."* The clear message is to keep trying, apply your learning and never give up.

- You realise that perhaps you need to take a different route to achieve your goal. Positive people aren't afraid of setbacks or admitting they are wrong, because they embrace and understand the learning process. Imagine what a joy every classroom would be if all students understood and enjoyed the learning process?

The last, and exciting thing to take away from having a win/learn mentality, is that it allows you to have better control of your emotions. When you adopt a positive mindset and attitude, you understand that a failure is not you or part of your identity. It is just an action that didn't go quite as you had hoped.

It is helpful to remember that you will grow and be successful if you keep taking action, learn, and persevere just as Thomas Edison did. Your persistence will pay off in the end no matter how long it takes. Will there be challenging days? Yes, there probably will be; however, you will not let them become the ruler of your behaviour, actions, and outcomes.

### Control the controllable
In life, we have little control of external circumstances, for example, we can't control the weather, the economy, the government, the education department or other people (no matter how much we would like this). Spending time worrying about these things is a waste of mental energy and can lead

people to feel disempowered. It can also reduce their physical energy and health.

In reality, we can only control how we respond to these external circumstances. As a teacher, you can help students understand this and enable them to influence their outcomes positively by working on what they can control rather than what they can't. When we have this mindset, we can more easily concentrate our efforts on achieving our goals.

### Single focus of champions

In our work with elite athletes and Olympians, we have come to recognise the power of single focus. Many people will say that they can multitask and do many things at the same time. Our experience, both physically and mentally, and the research of others[2], has demonstrated that every additional area that a person focuses their attention on, reduces their efficiency and accuracy. This should be obvious, as you are sharing your capability and capacity across multiple tasks.

The truly great champions focus on one thing at a time and give it a 100% of their attention. Of course, you can change your focus, but doing one thing at a time is the best way to achieve exceptional performance and maximise productivity. Think of the times when you have tried to juggle many things at once and the effect it had on you, your outcome, and particularly the additional stress it might have caused.

As a classroom teacher, can you encourage your students to learn to focus 100% of their attention on one thing at a time? This will enhance and develop the right mindset.

---

2 Examples of this research are included in our list of references on page 209.

## Using affirmations

1. Affirmations are a way of promoting positive thinking and if you follow this process, it will help you to create a positive mind. The simplest way to start writing affirmations is to **write a series of "I am" statements, which** describe what you want to have or experience.

   "I am confident"
   "I am optimistic"
   "I am feeling positive"

   Notice that we did not use the phrases "I want" or "I would like to" because these are just wishes. The mind works in the now and if you tell it that you are confident, it will believe you.

   To aid the process, it is helpful to close your eyes and imagine that you are already experiencing confidence, optimism, or positivity.

2. **Write your affirmations in the positive.**
   Write your affirmations in such a way, that they focus on what you want, rather than what you are trying to avoid or eliminate from your life.

   For example, rather than writing "I don't want to fail," convert this to "I want to succeed, and then to "I am successful." Or, "I would like to be fitter," to "I take regular exercise."

   Here's another example: Rather than writing, "I am trying to make friends," change it to a more positive choice such as, "I have a great support group."

   Even if it is not true at the moment, your mind thinks that it is and works to that principle.

3. **Write your affirmations in the NOW.**
When you write your affirmations, write them in the present tense, as though you are experiencing what you want *right now.*

Avoid phrases like, "I will be confident in the future." Why? Because the future state may never come. Everything that happens in life happens now, not in the past or the future, so focus your thoughts on the now. Use your affirmations to create an inner experience of having what you desire now.

"I am confident in speaking to others." and "I am unique and talented."

Notice that these two example affirmations make no reference to dates or times. They are simple and powerful affirmations of how you are right now.

4. **Write your affirmations with enthusiasm and feeling!**
It is really powerful when you use all your senses in creating an affirmation. This is because your imagination is a powerful tool and the more that you can add sounds and feelings to your words, the more powerful they will become.

For example, you could say, "I am feeling really optimistic as I stand up straight and talk with confidence to my friends, and hear them say how much I support them."

If you want to know how to write affirmations that are really effective, keep this in the front of your mind. When you describe your feelings about your affirmations, you connect with them more deeply and *they will have more power for you, if you experience them on both a thinking and feeling level.*

Listening to music while you recite your affirmations can also be of great benefit.  Music helps to engage your emotions, so that you are more able to tap into the feeling of what you wish to affirm.  Try listening to some music you find inspirational or relaxing, whatever helps to get you 'in the zone'.

5. **Don't get caught up in the "How"**
   When you are setting your affirmations, you don't need to worry about how you are going to make them happen.  Just be specific in what you want and once you have given your mind the suggestion, it starts to work automatically on getting the outcomes you want.

6. **Affirm your current successes as well!**
   Your affirmations don't all have to be about things that you want or that are currently absent from your life.  Consider your positive attributes and what is already working well for you.  Think about what you like about yourself and what you already have.  Include these in your affirmations.

7. So often we forget to give ourselves credit for the things that we like about ourselves and what we already do well, so when writing affirmations, do describe some of these things that you already appreciate about yourself and your life.  By doing so you will reinforce your positive feelings about who you are today, and you will be more open to accepting affirmations that describe who you would like to become.

**Write affirmations about ANYTHING!**
Think about what you would really like to change about yourself and your life, and be confident about affirming these.

- What thinking patterns or perceptions would you like to change?

- What circumstances would you like to improve or transform?

- What experiences would you like to have?

- What feelings would you like to enjoy?

- What do you want your life to be like?

8. **You can use affirmations to effect change on many different levels**, so take a moment to think about not only the things that you want, but also the experiences you would like to have, and the way you would like to feel about them. You can choose to manifest whatever you want in life!

Three more tips on how to write **supercharged affirmations**!

If you find that, some of your affirmations are difficult for you to believe, consider adding, "I choose" to them. For example, rather than writing "I am fit and healthy," you could write, "I choose to eat well and to exercise today."

It's a great idea to express gratitude in your affirmations. Consider starting some of them with the words, "I am so happy and grateful that..."

Another idea for writing affirmations that work on a deep level to transform your thinking patterns is to write about your expectations. Here's an example: "I expect to be successful in everything I do." This feels quite different to an affirmation of, "I am successful in everything I do."

Every now and then you may find yourself writing affirmations that feel like a stretch of the imagination. Perhaps you like the sound of it but you find it difficult to buy into. Writing about what you expect to happen, helps to dissolve any underlying doubts you may have about your affirmations and is a powerful technique for writing successful ones.

## Success Stories

There are many inspiring stories, of how people have used a positive mindset to achieve great things, despite them seeming impossible. They happen every day to people from all walks of life. A success story about positive mindset will often focus on someone who refused to accept negative results, and kept going despite frustrations and setbacks.

### JK Rowling: author of the Harry Potter series of books

Joanne Rowling was born in 1965 in Yate, Gloucestershire, England. As a child, Rowling often wrote fantasy stories, which she frequently read to her sister. Rowling has said that her teenage years were unhappy. Her home life was complicated by her mother's illness and a strained relationship with her father. She later said that she based the character of Hermione Granger on herself when she was eleven.

Sean Harris, her best friend in the Upper Sixth, owned a turquoise Ford Anglia, which she says inspired the flying version that appeared in *Harry Potter and the Chamber of Secrets*. She listened to two bands, the Smiths and the Clash, studied A-levels in English, French, and German, achieving two As and a B and was also Head Girl.

In 1982, she took the entrance exams for Oxford University, but was not accepted and read for a BA in French and Classics at the University of Exeter. She graduated in 1986 and moved to London to work as a researcher and bilingual secretary for Amnesty International.

In 1990, while she was on a four-hour delayed train trip from Manchester to London, the idea for a story of a young boy attending a school of wizardry "came fully formed" into her mind.

Rowling's mother Anne died after suffering from multiple sclerosis for ten years. Rowling was writing *Harry Potter* at the time and had never told her mother about the story, and her death heavily affected her writing. She then introduced greater detail of Harry's loss of his parents in the first book, because she knew how it felt.

Seven years after graduating from university, Rowling saw herself as a failure. Her marriage had failed, and she was jobless with a dependent child, but she also described this time as liberating and allowing her to focus on writing. During this period she was diagnosed with clinical depression and her illness inspired the characters known as Dementors, the soul-sucking creatures introduced in the third book. Rowling signed up for welfare benefits, describing her economic status as being as, "Poor as it is possible to be in modern Britain, without being homeless."

It took her many attempts before she could get a publisher to publish her first book. However, she believed in her characters in the book and continued to focus on being positive despite her hardship. She eventually wrote seven books in the Harry Potter series, which have been turned into films and as a result, she is now estimated to be a billionaire.

This is a story of hardship and at times heartbreak, but believing in herself and using her ability, J K Rowling proved to the world that if you have a dream and keep positive you could succeed.

### Debra Searle MVO MBE
Determined to succeed in a long-cherished dream, Debra Searle and her then husband Andrew, entered the Atlantic

Rowing Race, considered to be one of the toughest endurance events in the world. They were to race against 34 other double-handed crews, rowing 3000 miles from Tenerife to Barbados and were the only mixed-sex team in the event (the others were all male).

Despite previously having competed in rowing at an international level, Andrew very quickly discovered he was suffering from acute anxiety and had an irrational fear of the open ocean. They tried to work through this but after nine days, it became clear that he wasn't going to make it and a rescue yacht was called. Five days later, Andrew left their rowing boat.

Debra had a choice – get off the boat and join her husband or to go it alone. Three other crews had already been left solo, but none of them had lasted more than a few days alone.

This situation forced Debra to face up to a change that she hadn't expected or chosen. She knew others were thinking she couldn't possibly complete the journey on her own, but what was important was that she believed she could.

Debra had rehearsed parting with her husband by playing 'movies' in her mind, visualising what was going to happen, and so when the day came, it felt like she had already had the experience and knew the outcome. She was mentally prepared for the moment when Andrew would sail away, leaving her completely alone in their 23' plywood rowing boat.

As a novice rower (her husband was the professional), Debra obviously worried about the journey and the dangers she faced. Would a shark attack her? Would she be run over by a supertanker? Or perhaps be washed out of her small boat by a wave?

The race was intended to take around 60 days, but with only one of the two rowers remaining, it was likely to take much longer. Progress was sometimes slow. Debra talks about one three-day period, where she moved forward 20 miles, only for a strong headwind to knock her back 30 miles in one night!

One hundred and eleven days later, Debra successfully rowed into Barbados, with her family, support team, and hundreds of others standing on the quayside to greet her.

What was it that enabled her to overcome her lack of experience and the challenges of being alone for such a long period? She had to develop strategies and techniques to help her make it through this incredible journey. These included:

- **Visualisation**. We have already mentioned above how she played out the scene when her husband left on the rescue boat and she repeated this technique throughout her voyage. Playing the movie of her arrival in Barbados, was one example of how Debra kept the oars in motion and continued forward, even when she felt alone and exhausted.

- **Support team**. Debra realised that she couldn't do it on her own and had to learn to ask for help. As she approached Christmas she realised she didn't want to spend it alone and in the boat. But her twin sister had other ideas, telling her that they weren't ready for her to give up yet and arranging for a yacht to deliver some goodies for her.

  Debra also kept an on-line diary, and when she was starting to feel very lonely this was connected to a mobile phone provider's website and anybody could follow her story in her diary and send her short text messages too. She very quickly received over 1000 of them, and they gave her a massive boost. These words were free and gave enormous encouragement and also helped Debra to realise the choice she had in using her own words to encourage herself and others. Debra speaks about her realisation of the power of words – how we are given an infinite amount of words to say each day, which are completely 'free', and yet are so powerful.

She's not even sure that she would have successfully completed the row had it not been for the encouraging words of her friends, family, and even complete strangers. She is now aware of how she uses her free words to build others up every day.

- **Having a passionate belief** that she would make it, even when others doubted her.

All the above support the steps we have covered so far in this book.

The biggest of all though, was the realisation that she could choose her attitude every day.

Debra created a 'choose your attitude' exercise that she completed at the start of each day, choosing a word to describe the attitude she was going to role model, for example, "Today I will be optimistic." Then she would list all the reasons that the day would be an optimistic one.

This is a technique that Debra still applies today and as a result she achieves more of the outcomes she seeks and it underpins her continued success.

Being self-aware and having a positive mindset is a big step in building resilience.

If you aren't already doing this, why not try it and see how it changes your daily outcomes, and those for your students.

**Tom's story**
Tom was a young professional, who felt fortunate to have

succeeded in getting a very sought after job. He was chosen from over a hundred people vying for the position in technical sales and was thrilled. He really thought he'd made it and was on his way to a reliable career.

Two weeks into his new job, Tom noticed that everyone around him complained a lot. Nobody seemed to enjoy going to work or what they did. He didn't understand this, as he really liked his job and the company.

Someone would say, "Hi Tom. How are you today?"

Tom would reply, "Great. And you?"

Then they'd respond back with something like, "Just wait until you're here a bit longer. You won't say that anymore." They'd laugh like it was a joke, but they clearly meant it. Tom had found out that his dream job was within a culture that was full of negativity. The people he worked with were talented and good at what they did, but they seemed content to walk around with an apathetic attitude day in and day out. The situation led Tom to have a serious talk with himself about continuing to work at the company. He only really had two choices: stay or go.

Talking about it with his wife, Tom shared everything he was thinking about. He explained the culture and the people he saw every day, but he also knew that he really loved what he did.

She looked at him and smiled, taking in everything he had to say. She asked, "Why can't you try to change their habits?"

"What do you mean? I can't go in and just make everyone there think differently?"

"You can't force them to, but you can lead by example. From what you say, they're taken aback by your positive nature. Why not keep using it and show them that they have the option to become more positive as well. It just isn't a one way street."

Tom smiled, thinking this would be really hard but it felt right for him to try. Over the next few days, he placed positive sayings on his workstation. People made some negative comments, but he said that it helped him keep positive and be grateful for the job he loved to do.

For a while people were suspicious of him, thinking he was up to something. He didn't go overboard, but he was himself. In time, he found out that people did start responding more positively to him. Better yet, he could hear others making more positive comments to each other and wearing a smile on their face Things began to change and it really did stem from Tom. A positive mindset and attitude can be just as contagious as a negative one. You may have to work a bit harder, but you can get results nonetheless.

Imagine the lives you can impact through positive thoughts and actions every day and understand how much power the positive thoughts and actions have over you, others, and the environment. They have real value. Through Tom's realisation of this, he made a difference to a work environment that appeared to be set in its ways. And since the work environment often affects the home environment, he probably made a big difference in the personal lives of some of those he worked with too. A positive outlook on life is one of the greatest gifts you can share with others.

## Thought Momentum

Teachers have a unique opportunity to see how their students embrace different ideas and situations. Unlike adults, young people are often more open-minded and less cynical. They may already have some negative thoughts and behaviours, but these are easier to change because they are not so ingrained. Establishing the benefits of positive thinking can really make the difference. It allows for students to:

- Be more open to learning.
- Overcome initial setbacks.
- Develop empathy and understanding.
- Look for opportunities.
- Create a personal ethos that is based on positive thought and action.

As for you, the teacher, you will be rewarded with students who:

- Are more excited to learn new things.
- Work better together and are more considerate of each other's differences and needs.
- Have greater determination to complete tasks.
- Are able to think creatively, resourcefully, and confidently.

Everybody wins when a positive mindset becomes part of a group's culture inside and outside of the classroom.


## Taking the Next Step

Teaching young people to believe in their abilities, to have confidence, and to address life with a positive approach is important, because these are the foundations of success and they help build resilience.

A great way to open up the conversation about positive mindset is to talk about Henry Ford's quote:

 *Whether you think you can or think you can't, you are right."*

The above quote is also known as a self-fulfilling prophecy and provides a valuable lesson. When students realise that what they think and verbalise often comes true, they will be more interested in thinking positively about what they want in their lives.

Start with your students in small groups to discuss the above Henry Ford quote. Give everyone a chance to respond and let them share what it means to them.

Ask them to talk about experiences they had, when they said to themselves 'yes I can' or 'no I can't' do something and discuss the result.

After they share their examples, you can add yours, letting them know when you thought you could and couldn't do something and found out you were right in both cases.

Use two or three examples of where people didn't try something, because they thought they couldn't and talk about what would have happened if they addressed those situations with a positive mindset. Ask questions such as:

- What stopped you from trying?
- What is the worst thing that could have happened?
- What did you think later about not attempting this?
- Were other people encouraging you to try (or not)?
- What would you do differently today if you had the chance again?

- What would you say to yourself to ensure that you have a go next time, or with other new opportunities?

Young people are very honest when they get into these discussions. Sometimes, it can be a small thing that stopped them from pursuing their goal or taking a chance. You can show them that it's okay to have these doubts and challenges and with a different mindset, they can change things in the future.

**Remember that past performance is not an indicator of future success!**
Referring to the concept of win/lose versus win/learn, students can understand that there are good lessons to be learned from something not initially working out the way they would have liked. You can complete the following exercises.

1) Decide on a scenario to talk through with your class to compare win/lose and win/learn scenarios. Here are a few ideas for you:

   a. Suzie tries out for a school sports team, but does not make it.

   b. Dan gets a lower grade on his test than the one he wanted, despite studying the night before while watching TV.

   c. Jennifer tried to make some new friends but had no luck.

   d. Sam has lost his last three competitive games of tennis.

2) Whether you choose a scenario above or one of your own, you can discuss what happens if you follow the more usual win/lose approach. You can also cover:

    **a.** What thoughts do you experience when you do not succeed?

    **b.** How do you feel emotionally?

    **c.** What might this mean for your learning and whether or not you try again?

    **d.** If you accept that you lost, or didn't get what you wanted, what affect did this have on your mindset and resilience?

**3)** Now it's time to discuss how situations can become win/learn if you have the right positive mindset. This is where students build their resilience and it starts with their thinking. You might like to discuss ideas such as:

    **a.** What might you do when you don't achieve what you want?

    **b.** How can you reframe your thinking to focus on the learning and possibilities?

    **c.** What are the differences when you embrace win/learn compared to win/lose?

    **d.** What has happened in your life recently, where you can take what could have become a win/lose situation and turn it into win/learn? (This is a good time for the students to write down their experiences. They do not necessarily have to share it with the class unless they wish to.)

We have already mentioned that every person has a voice in their head – self talk. It helps guide people to make choices in their lives. Your self talk can focus on both positive and negative thoughts, depending on how a person has been conditioned. For example, some people see the world as a glass half full or a glass half empty. If you see the world as half full, your self talk says things like 'I can' or 'that's possible', while a glass half empty person says in their mind 'I can't' or 'that's not possible' for someone like me.

With the following exercise it's important to get students to reflect about how they actually think. This involves them realising that their thinking has an impact on the results they get. Another example you could give of a negative voice in their head would be:

> *I'd really love to take art class, but I'm no good at drawing. I shouldn't do it. I don't want to embarrass myself."*

Follow that up with examples of how a student could use positive thinking and self talk.

> *I'd really love to take art class. It may be a challenge but I choose to have that experience and improve my skills."*

There is a significant difference between these two voices, with one more likely to lead to success and the other talking you out of being successful (even if in both examples they have the same skills and abilities).

If you see the world as half full, your self talk says things like 'I can' or 'that's possible', while a glass half empty person says in their mind 'I can't' or 'that's not possible' for someone like me.

Ask the students to think of some words and phrases that would constitute negative self talk. Here are some examples of words that should be avoided, if students want to develop a positive mindset.

- I can't.
- I shouldn't.
- I'm not good enough.
- I don't have the energy.
- I'm hopeless.
- The situation is hopeless.
- They would never let me.
- I'm useless and no good at anything.

Then ask them to come up with words or phrases that would be more helpful and positive. There are some examples below that can lead to a student affirming that they are very capable:

- I can.
- I will.
- It is possible.
- That interests me.
- I choose to experience that.
- I am having fun and enjoying myself.
- I expect to try new things.
- Let's give it a try.

From there, you can have a discussion about how much better positive self talk makes you feel. It can turn an average day into a good day, a challenging situation into a learning one. To support students in switching their thoughts to positive driven actions and emotions, it will also be helpful for them to know the triggers that drive negative self talk.

Ask students to consider their self talk (particularly when they are in difficult situations or when they are stepping out of their comfort zone). Is it positive or negative? What ideas do they have to make positive thinking a good habit? Here are some ideas you can share.

- When they go into a stressful or new situation be aware of their self talk. If it is negative then change it and replace it with some positive thoughts like 'I can' or 'I will'.

- Keep a diary or write a note about the good things they do.

- At the end of each day, ask them to think of and write down three things (positively framed) that they have done well that day. These can be anything, as long as they feel positive about them. A piece of work or test score, something nice they did for a friend, some sport they played, a joke they told that made others laugh. You could do this in the last class of each day.

- During individual lessons or classes you can ask questions that help them become and stay more positive. What have you learned? What did you do well? How did you overcome that obstacle?

- When we help young people develop these as everyday habits they will start to use them.

Ask who else can help them to develop positive self talk. It could be a teacher, parent or friend.

Dr Barbara Fredrickson, in her book 'Positivity', revealed the real impact of positive and negative self talk through her research[3]. She said that negative self talk closes down both the heart and the mind, and leads to lower levels of performance, enjoyment, and learning, while positive self talk does the opposite and allows people to flourish and grow.

She identified a positivity ratio of 3:1 and found that people needed at least three pieces of positive self talk to every negative one, if they are going to build their self-esteem, confidence, and resilience. The above suggestions will help support young people in developing the right positive habits.

Another way of supporting students is through identifying and building on their strengths. Everyone has natural strengths and talents that are easier to develop and it is more effective to spend time and effort on them, as it will build a sense of achievement. In work, managers often spend all their time trying to develop the weak areas of those they lead and this is not the most effective use of time or course of action. Helping people find work in those areas they enjoy and where their strengths are a real asset, brings far greater reward. Adopting this practice while people are still young is a great service you can give.

> *"Everyone has natural strengths and talents that are easier to develop and it is more effective to spend time and effort on them, as it will build a sense of achievement."*

3  See the list of references on page 209 for details of Barbara Fredrickson's research on positivity.

Once people have grown in one area of expertise, they can take the learning and enthusiasm into other areas. This is a great way to help students revisit what makes them strong and how being successful in one thing can support them in others.

The following exercises will help students pinpoint their greatest assets.

**What are your strengths? What can you do?**
Ask them to write down their perceived strengths (what they are good at) and what they can do, even if only a little. They should end up with quite a long list, because most people can do a little in many areas even if they are not true strengths. When they have their list, ask them to work with a partner and share their strengths and the things they can do with each other.

This is a great way to get students thinking widely, because they'll also find benefits in what the student they are sharing with has to say, perhaps even uncovering something that is a strength of theirs, but they didn't realise it. You can ask those that are willing, to share with the class and add your own stories as well.

**How can you use your strengths to build and maintain a positive mindset and to achieve the things that you want?**
Ask your students to think about how their strengths underpin a positive mindset. After their discussion, give each student a chance to state their top tip for keeping a positive mindset.

**What are you going to do differently as a result of these exercises?**
Ask your students to take positive action for doing something differently for themselves. Have them write down one step they will take and then follow this up to monitor their progress.

One of the best things about these exercises is that as students practise these new skills and behaviours, their thinking will naturally become more positive.

Step six to resilience is Positive Mindset -  make it your daily habit!

 *Once you replace negative thoughts with positive ones, you'll start having positive results."*
~ Willy Nelson ~

# CHAPTER NINE: THE SEVEN STEPS – NUMBER 7 PHYSICAL ACTION

*We are what we repeatedly do. Excellence, therefore, is not an act but a habit."*
~ Aristotle ~

Physical action can be divided into two parts. Firstly, we need to be physically healthy and energised in order to be successful and secondly, we need to take action. There is a saying that a vision without action is but a dream. In this chapter we examine both aspects of physical action and the importance of developing the right habits.

## Physical Health

How we treat our bodies has an impact on everything we do. Active people have considerably more energy than those who take little or no physical exercise. It's not just about exercise; it's also how you take care of your body. Well-being isn't about physical perfection or an ideal body image; it's about looking after your body so that it can serve you best, giving you the ability to do the things you want to do every day. Having good physical health and energy is also important in building resilience and overcoming setbacks. Imagine how you feel when you are hungry, tired and lack energy. Your physical state has a direct impact on your emotions and your mental state. A strong body leads to a strong mind.

If you want you and your students to achieve great things, you have to pay attention to what's at the centre of all action – you. Positive thoughts as we learned in the last chapter are important, but you also need to have a physical body that is able to respond to your needs. Great ideas cannot be acted out when you're physically tired. It is just not possible. You may be able to push through and persevere for a day or two, but you will fizzle out in the long run.

As a teacher, you are likely to have seen students who are clearly tired day after day, obviously not getting enough sleep or rest. Or perhaps have no energy because they don't have a healthy diet. Teachers cannot control what their students do at home or at school, but they can lead by example. This might include effective energy management. In this chapter, you will discover some tools to help your students realise that they can develop more energy by making smart choices on a daily basis and when they are energised they can commit to action and get the results they want.

## Learning Outcomes

As you go through the steps in this chapter you will learn about two very important aspects of physical action and how it relates to every person, regardless of age.

1. **Successful people build energy through physical activity and create healthy balanced lifestyles.**
   Physical activity extends beyond just improving movement and plays an important role in aspects of a person's well-being and resilience such as:

   - Stress levels.

   - Health.

   - The ability to handle situations.

   - Attitude.

   - Confidence.

   - Having a positive outlook.

Poor lifestyle choices seldom have immediate impact, they tend to creep up on you and before you realise it, you're exhausted and things feel out of control. You might ask yourself, "How did things get this way?" Then you find yourself wondering, "How was it so easy to get to this point, yet so challenging to change?"

The good news is that your students have the opportunity to learn good habits while they are still young.

2. **Successful people take action.**
   The first step of any journey begins with thinking about the destination or where you want to go. The key to making this a reality is taking action. Motivation on its own is not enough. As human beings, we also need to use our willpower, to make choices and take action. We will explore this in more detail in this chapter.

## Energise your Way to Exceptional Performance and Results

There are steps that can be taken on a daily basis, to increase your energy levels and so build your resilience and ensure that you are doing the things that lead towards growth and success. When you make a committed effort to do these things, you'll find that your personal and professional life improves. Students will also make improvements in their personal life and achieve greater academic success.

Every day there are physical demands placed on you. Imagine this as being your energy demand – just like a house that needs heating and maintenance to keep its inhabitants warm and safe. To get the most out of your life, you need to match and balance this need with your supply of energy. You need to make regular energy deposits (food and drink), as you don't want to run out of fuel before all your tasks are done.

*The first step of any journey begins with thinking about the destination or where you want to go. The key to making this a reality is taking action.*

Here are eight tips to help you and your students find your way to better physical health and a balanced lifestyle,

Tip number one: *Stay hydrated all day long.*

Dehydration is taxing on the body and the mind, and is one of the main causes of tiredness. If you think of your body as a battery, without liquid it doesn't hold a positive charge. It is recommended to:

- Drink two to five litres of water on a daily basis (depending on your height, weight and the exercise you give your body).

- Have water whenever you are feeling tired. It provides you with energy while increasing your concentration.

- When you first feel hungry or you have the need to eat something in a rush (particularly if you have already eaten within a reasonable time period), drink a glass of water first. It is often an early sign that you are dehydrating.

For students: Encourage them to have a water bottle with them if it's allowed in your school. Otherwise, suggest they get a drink if they seem to be losing focus. It will give them both movement and water, two great things for energy.

Tip number two: *Ensure you move regularly during the day.*

Human beings were designed to move and not be sedentary. Movement on a frequent basis, at least hourly, is good for you on every level. It allows your body to stretch out, increases oxygen flow, and gives your mind and eyes a rest from the task you are undertaking, whether that is using your computer, books, or other activities. Movement is great for increasing concentration and productivity.

Here are things you can consider doing:

- Find a reason to move hourly. Even if it is just stretching at your desk. Locate things so you have to move; for example, don't have your printer on your desk or drinks to hand. Make sure you have to walk a little to get them. For those of you teaching, you do get to move during and between lessons (as will many of your students).

- Regularly break from what you are doing and take several deep breaths to re-energise and focus yourself.

- Purchase a pedometer and commit to trying to take 10,000 steps daily. That is the recommended number of steps you should take each day for better health.

- Set your phone alarm to remind you to get up and move.

- Make sure you do take a break for lunch and as well as eating, find time to do something you really enjoy, whether that might be reading a book, listening to music, going for a walk or whatever your favourite pastime might be.

Encourage your students to move, and you may be able to incorporate some movement into your lessons too. Be creative!

Tip number three: *Ensure you take regular exercise.*

Exercise can be seen as only for those who like sport, whereas if we want to be healthy and energised, we all need to take some form of exercise. It doesn't have to be formal or a team activity. It's more a matter of ensuring you exercise your muscles and importantly your heart. Exercise can be a simple walk – as long as you get slightly out of breath – or you might try dancing or riding a bicycle. Whatever you enjoy doing.

Fitness experts tell us that having at least three sessions of twenty-minutes exercise that raise your heartbeat each week is what is needed. Any exercise is better than no exercise, so ask your students to identify something that they enjoy and to work out how it can become part of their everyday lives.

Tip number four: *Keep a regular sleep schedule.*

It's much easier to get a good night's rest when you go to sleep at the same time every night and get the recommended amount of sleep that you need (seven/eight hours for most people and often more for younger people). It's a good idea to work out your best sleep pattern, keeping in mind that too much sleep is not better than too little. It's all about balance. Some things to do to help the quality of your sleep include:

- Be quiet before bedtime, and avoid over stimulating activities such as video games or exercise.

- Avoid caffeine or other stimulants in the evening, because they do interrupt sleep for many people.

- Enjoy a healthy snack sometime ahead of going to bed, which helps you drift off to a peaceful night's sleep.

- Ensure that you have a quiet bedroom, if possible.

For students, it's about raising their awareness and tying this in with their agenda and what they want to achieve. The young often rebel, want to stay up later or don't think about these things (and why would they)? Helping them to understand the impact they are having on their own performance and linking it with what they want to get out of life, is the way to motivate them.

Tip number five: *Make sure that you eat regularly.*

You wouldn't set off on a long car journey without filling up the petrol tank. Yet how many people go without food (particularly breakfast), or if they do eat, they do so at irregular intervals.

The latest medical evidence shows that in order to keep our sugar/ glucose levels at an optimum level to keep working effectively, we need to eat every 2/3 hours. Research suggests that we should eat three main meals a day with small healthy snacks in between[4]. It's also important to remember that breakfast is the most important meal of the day, as it's difficult to work and have energy on an empty stomach.

Tip number six: *Make sure you eat quality food.*

Not only do you need to eat regularly, but also the quality of what you eat has an effect on your energy levels. That isn't to say that we can't eat treats or always have to eat only healthy foods, but it's sometimes helpful to use Pareto's 80/20 rule. That is to say you can eat quality food 80% of the time and 20% of the time, eat things you like that might not make it onto the latest healthy food guide.

Ask your students what they think is healthy versus less healthy foods (less healthy foods have high levels of fat, sugar or salt, such as cakes, fizzy drinks, and crisps, while healthy foods include fruit and vegetables). This isn't a health food guide and you will have lots of resources in schools that will help you. The key is to link this back to the students' interests and how they can increase their energy levels to help achieve the things *they* want.

---

4 See the list of references on page 210 for sources of research relating to eating habits and blood/glucose levels.

<u>Tip number seven</u>: *Make sure you have variety in your day.*

There is an old saying that all work and no play makes Jack a dull boy. The secret to having a healthy lifestyle is to have a balance of different activities. Of course, putting in effort to achieve academic success is important and having time to make friends and taking time out to exercise and pursue hobbies makes life more interesting.

<u>Tip number eight</u>: *Avoid drugs and limit your alcohol intake.*

There is often peer pressure or opportunities for young people to try or use drugs, or alcohol, and adults can also use them to provide enjoyment, support or to escape from challenges. They provide artificial stimuli and reduce energy and focus and you will already have programmes to educate your students in this area. Help students to understand how using alcohol or drugs might affect the long-term achievement of their goals, as well as the enjoyment of those things in which they have the greatest interest.

So can improved physical activity and personal wellbeing improve academic performance? In their book, 'Spark!', Dr John J. Ratey and Eric Hagerman[5] tell the story of a movement, which began near Chicago in 1990, and subsequently spread across the school district and then into other districts within the US.

They reference wider research undertaken to study the impact of physical activity, which demonstrates a correlation between improved activity and higher academic performance. What they show is that teaching young people how to manage their fitness and better look after themselves, has a direct impact on their overall school performance.

---

5 See the list of references on page 211 for details of the book Spark! How exercise will improve the performance of your brain.

In addition, they suggest that raising the heart rate and taking some physical activity at the start of a school day, improves concentration and performance. They provide evidence to back up the points they make and anyone with an interest in this subject, would find the investment in their book worthwhile.

## Physical Action

We have now shared some ideas about ways to build physical energy and the next step is to think about how we use this energy to fulfil our hopes and dreams. We are called human beings and while just being who you are is good, we are also programmed to want to achieve things in life. For most people, the hardest step in moving forward is just to take action, as we often put things off to another day or we just don't start at all.

This is when our motivation needs to be converted into action using our willpower. Recent research has suggested that we only have a limited amount of willpower[6] and the difference that allows us to take action is forming good habits. Much of what we do every day is done unconsciously. You probably don't think too much about brushing your teeth in the morning or even getting dressed and getting to work, it's just automatic. You have formed habits where you just get things done.

**Here are five tips on taking action.**

Tip number one: *Make sure you have a clear goal and purpose each and every day.*

It's easy to go off track, especially when something else really catches your attention or your task for the day seems rather dull or difficult. Jumping from one thing to another or putting off something, uses up valuable energy and sabotages performance.

---

6  See the list of references on page 211 for details of research that suggests willpower is a limited resource.

**Every 1000 mile journey**

**starts with a first step.**

Planning (step four of building resilience), makes the tasks you need to do daily, more manageable, and achievable. You can clearly see each step that needs to be taken. If you allocate a time for these tasks at the beginning of your day or the night before, you stop all the internal chatter (self talk) about what you should do first.

This saves on energy and you will know exactly where you are heading and what needs to be done to get the results you want.

You can teach your students how to organise their days, so they are effectively using their time and not waiting until the last minute to do important things.

<u>Tip number two:</u> *Prioritise your day and complete one task at a time (single focus of champions) – always start with the most important ones* first.

Some people try to multitask or just jump back and forth from one thing to another. This may seem desirable, because you trick yourself into believing that you are taking care of more things at once. However, research[7] shows that you are:

- Doing more things less effectively.
- Draining energy.
- Unlikely to be achieving the results you want.

This is a great time to talk about examples for students, such as homework and school projects, showing them the value of focusing on one thing at a time before moving on to the next. Soon they'll realise that they will actually have more down time or fun time, if they concentrate on getting one thing done before moving on to the next.

<u>Tip number three:</u> *Take frequent mental breaks throughout the day as it will sustain your energy and productivity.*

A mental break doesn't have to be over an extensive period. It's designed to recharge you. It's particularly effective when you are feeling like you're being pulled in different directions, or you have been concentrating for a long time. During your break you could:

- Close your eyes for a few minutes and visualise something rejuvenating and exciting.
- Take a brief walk.

---

7   See the list of references on page 209 for details of the research showing multitasking reduces efficiency and performance.

- Stretch your body and breathe deeply.

- Meditate or daydream for a few minutes.

- Or do anything else you really enjoy.

If as a teacher you have an extended lesson, what can you do to have 'breaks'? Perhaps you could let students know that they can get up and stretch their legs if they need to, in order to restore their energy. It beats watching them yawn or seeing them stare into space!

Tip number four: *Control the controllable.*

As we have already covered previously, you can't control many things in life, for example the weather, the economy, your friends and family's moods or sometimes what subjects you have to study in school. What you can control is your attitude and your focus. If you want to achieve in your life, take action, which is aligned to what you do want, and to the things that you can control.

Teaching students about the things they can control – their attitude and where they focus their time and energy – will enable them to be more successful. In terms of attitude, it is important that they don't compare themselves with others and just work on being the best they can be.

Tip number five: *Embrace and grow your support team.*

This is one of the seven steps (number five) to building resilience and it also sits here as part of building physical action. Nobody has to go it alone, but many people think they have to or should do. You may drain your energy, optimism, and perspective if you think you have to do everything yourself, particularly when you face challenges, surround yourself with negative people or narrow your potential through having limiting beliefs.

Having the right support team not only reduces any energy drain, it refills your batteries and becomes a source of energy. A problem shared is often a problem halved.

Encourage your students to ask for help proactively, when it's necessary, and not to wait until they feel stuck or even hopeless. It will make all the difference to their outlook and productivity. Raising awareness of this and discussing how to build effective support groups, will significantly help your students. You might think about establishing support groups within classes or the school.


## Success Stories

We mentioned Thomas Edison in a previous chapter and over the course of his impressive career, he patented 1,093 inventions. One of the best known of those inventions is of course the first commercial electric light bulb.

Some people have blamed Thomas Edison for losing one to two hours of valuable sleep each night, because the artificial light tricked their bodies into thinking it was still daytime and there was more time to do things. For a man who was credited with statements saying that he regarded sleep as a waste of time, the light bulb was a perfectly logical and incredible invention (although you know how important sleep really is for most people).

The one thing that nobody knew about Thomas Edison was he was a power-napper. He knew full well that to do what he loved most, inventing and exploring new horizons, he had to have a clear mind. He knew that rest was important and that he was unlikely to keep moving forward with his ambitious 'to-do' list, without it.

Edison had beds set up all over his home and laboratory, so that whenever he needed to take a power nap he could. So, while he chose to get his needed rest in a different manner, he was very aware of how important sleep was and that without giving his genius and inventive mind a break during the day, his dreams, goals, and ambitions would not be achieved.

Edison is a great example of the importance of knowing yourself and understanding how your body functions at its best. We all have a natural clock and internal rhythm that we need to listen to in order to work and play at our best every day. Our goal may not to be an inventor, but we all have a desire to achieve things. It takes rest and resilience to make that happen.

**Nick Vujicic's** story is heart-warming and is likely to bring tears to your eyes if you watch one of his videos on YouTube, but not because you are sad for him. Nick was born without limbs and with limited physical ability, but he has shown the world that it is attitude and not aptitude that makes the biggest difference to being successful. He gives people the feel-good factor with his positivity, and his perspective on life is a good lesson for everyone to learn. He is a great example of someone who walks his talk, lives to his values every day and above all takes action.

There are few things that Nick won't attempt. He has played soccer, been diving, gone down water slides, and carved a career as an international speaker and much more. He lives his life to the full. He doesn't look at himself, as disabled or lacking ability, because he knows it is only he who defines his own limits. It's a message that he's taken to the streets and to schools, telling others about how he has found his own unique way to experience life, and that it has no limits. He doesn't want people's pity but to show them what might be possible in their lives. He says it's just a lie to think you're not good enough or not worth anything.

Nick's ability to touch others lives through his own, has given him opportunities to reach out to children and adults alike, letting them know that they have value and purpose. It's theirs for the finding and taking and they just need to:

- Be thankful for what they have,
- Dream big; and
- Believe in themselves, take action and never give up.

Through Nick's perspective, people can see that everyone is worth something and understanding this, gives the strength to conquer all that comes before you. Think about your own life. Be the hero in your dreams, and don't allow any shortcomings stop you from taking action and achieving your full potential.

## Thought Momentum

There are many ideas on how we should strive to be physically active and take action, but the key is taking the first steps. This is the only way we will see results.

So what can you do to sleep better, eat healthily (80/20), exercise regularly, make good choices, plan your life, and create good habits?

The first step is to raise awareness and you are hopefully becoming more aware as you read this book. Sharing these

*There are many ideas on how we should strive to be physically active and take action, but the key is taking the first steps. This is the only way we will see results.*

thoughts with your students, will enable them to think about some of the things they currently do and what they might do differently in the future. They could think about

- How much sleep they currently get and how much they need?

- How healthily they eat?

- How too much sugar might affect their mood?

- How much energy they usually have?

- How much exercise they currently take and how much they really need?

- How effective they are at taking action to help them achieve their goals?

- What are their current habits and what new habits could they create, to help them be more successful?

Even though you cannot control what happens outside the classroom, you can help students understand what they can do to be more effective.


## Taking the Next Step

Resilience is much easier, when you are physically energised and mentally prepared to manage everyday challenges, and students will benefit from developing good habits that they can carry with them through life. As your students become more aware and responsible for their own good habits, they are more likely to self–adjust when they are tempted to veer off course.

One exercise you might like to take with your students is to ask them how physical activity affects resilience. You can start by asking your students:

Imagine you are tired, hungry, and thirsty. How might you feel and how does it affect your performance?

Some typical responses may include:

- They want to lie around or do nothing.
- They don't have energy for physical activities.
- They want to be left alone.
- They don't want to think or try to solve problems.
- They are short-tempered with others.
- They underperform or do badly at things they try.

Do share some of your own feelings and stories too. Now that students understand the typical responses when they are physical or mentally tired, you can begin to find solutions with them by asking:

When you feel like this how does it affect your resilience? They are likely to be far less resilient and when things go wrong, they won't have the same ability to bounce back.

Now you can ask: How can you make sure that you are in the best physical shape to be resilient?

Your students will have many ideas and some answers may include:

- Getting enough sleep.
- Eating well and not having too much fat, sugar or salt in their diet.
- Making sure they eat breakfast every day.
- Drinking enough water throughout the day.
- Exercising daily in some way.

- Walking more.

- Knowing how drugs and alcohol can take away physical energy and cause short and long-term harm.

- Keeping a journal of their good habits.

- 80/20 rule: it is okay to have treats at times, but keep a good balance, making them the exception rather than the rule.

Have the students write down what they feel they currently do well, in their day-to-day lives. Then ask them to pick one more that they could improve on, or start doing.

This will help them to start creating a new habit. Through questioning, you can help them understand why the changes they suggest are good and what it will take to make it a habit. You can support this by going through four key factors and asking them:

1) *What is your reason to change?* Think of one powerful reason why the change you want is good for you.

2) *What values does this reason support?* Students need to identify with the values that will underpin the change they seek. For example: honesty, self-respect, better health, greater achievement, etc. Ask them to explain what values might be important to them in making the change.

3) *What is your plan to create the change?* Without making a plan, action is unlikely to follow.

4) *What action steps can you take today?* For both questions 3 and 4 use the G.R.O.W. model to ensure that a well thought out and personal plan, is put into place.

Once you are satisfied that your students have a clear goal and plan, ask them how they can make it as motivational as possible for themselves.  If their goal or plan doesn't inspire them to take action, they are unlikely to achieve it.  What can they add to make sure that it has real interest for them?

Step seven to building resilience is Physical Action – and it supports the other steps.

 *Physical fitness can neither be achieved by wishful thinking nor outright purchase."*
~ Joseph Pilates ~

# CHAPTER TEN: PUTTING IT ALL TOGETHER

*Do not let what you cannot do interfere with what you can do."*
~ John Wooden ~

The power to change your life doesn't come from what you've learned in this book. It comes from your ability to take the information and apply it to your life, allowing you to build new positive habits and pass these on to your students and colleagues.

Using the seven steps as a systematic step by step approach to building resilience for you and your students will show that you:

- Can put yourself in the <u>place</u> of most potential.
- Are full of <u>passion</u> when it comes to doing what excites you.
- Can realise your <u>purpose</u> and be proactive in achieving it.
- Have the means to access the <u>people</u> that want to help and support you.
- Are resourceful and setting goals and <u>planning</u> will ensure you are focused and effective.
- Can use your <u>positive mindset</u> to energise your drive for success.
- Must have physical well-being and take <u>action</u> to maximise your potential.

Are these steps always easy?

No.  However, they are worth pursuing.  With them you will make significant progress, build confidence and character, bounce back from setbacks and realise your full potential.

## The Sum of Success

The seven steps are designed to support teachers to help build resilience personally and in their students, by sharing valuable ideas and practical steps.

If you think about your dream classroom and students what might they look like?  Perhaps something like this?

They would be enthusiastic and energised young people with open minds.  Students would fully engage in lessons without fear and ask questions to satisfy their intellectual curiosity. When they looked at you, they would see someone who acted as a role model for success and resilience, and who they respected and looked to for leadership.

Use the seven steps to help create this environment and to build:

- Resilience.
- Confident and well balanced students.
- Fully engaged learners.
- Ambition & achievement.
- Positive attitudes.
- Self-belief.

It's easy to smile when you think of a world where all children have the opportunity for happiness and the ability to overcome obstacles in their lives.  Successful resilient children will make the world a better place for themselves and make a full contribution to the communities in which they live.

## Conclusion

 *Those who can truly be accounted brave are those who best know the meaning of what is sweet in life and what is terrible, and then go out, undeterred, to meet what is to come."*
~ Pericles ~

When you read the quote by Pericles above, you can substitute the word resilient for brave. Resilience is a characteristic that every teacher would like for their students and every parent wants for their child. We want young people to embrace challenge, to fulfil their potential, find success though focus and determination, and experience joy in an abundant life.

There are lots of challenges and information given to you every day, but in the end it all comes down to you and your mindset. You need to:

- Take responsibility for your actions and the changes you want to make.

And;

- Not allow yourself to be stifled by fear.
- And keep going when things get tough.

As a teacher, you are in a great position to support your students. You can explore techniques that will really change their mindset and make their experience with you, so much more enjoyable and productive. You can help them:

- Manage peer pressure.
- Extend their comfort zone and try new things.

- Become more self-confident through understanding how they think.

- Learn the valuable lessons that come from setbacks.

- Use their most powerful resources; their own mind, body, emotions and spirit (knowing their meaning and purpose).

Most adults have a natural tendency to want to love and protect their children. That is understandable, and the real challenge is to realise that children don't need to be wrapped in cotton wool. We can't prevent them from getting bumps, bruises, or having setbacks at times in their lives. In fact this is the way they grow and develop.

Wouldn't it be a greater gift to give them the tools that equip them for life – to enable them to have a growth mindset, be resilient, and truly fulfil their potential? The seven steps will help you do this – Place, Passion, Purpose, People, Planning, Positive mindset, and Physical action.

Our request to you is to adopt these steps and share the insights to help young people build the positive habits and resilience that will serve them well for their whole lives.

If you would like some specific lesson resources designed to build resilience and other life skills, then we have over 50 one-hour lessons (and 100 hours of activities) available in our resilience and employability curriculum, which will enable you to work directly with students. These include full lesson plans, student worksheets, classroom PowerPoint presentations and some supporting videos.

You can find out more by contacting us using the details at the end of this chapter, or by visiting www.successfullives.co.uk.

These lessons are built on over 20 years of experience, developing already successful people and helping them to change unhelpful habits and build new ones. We decided, that in addition to doing this, it would be much more powerful and satisfying, to use our knowledge and expertise to support young people in developing the good habits in the first place, and that they could use this knowledge and expertise for their successful lives.

As an additional chapter below, we have shared some of our experience and lessons on developing coaching in young people. This is another way of helping to build resilience and supports using the GROW model, which we have already introduced. It also allows your students to become their own high performance coaches, which will accelerate their results.

Often coaching in schools appears to be seen as a remedial intervention. Yet in business and sport it is usually the highly successful people or those identified as having high potential that pay to have a coach?

They realise getting support from someone else and becoming good at asking themselves the right questions, lets them have greater clarity on their goals and ultimately brings better results.

The final chapter below is followed by a quick guide to the seven steps and the exercises you can use with your students to build resilience, so you have a fast way to recap or find information you need.

Thank you for sharing our book and we are always looking to learn and develop ourselves, so we welcome your feedback. What have you found helpful, what can we improve upon and what success stories can you share?

Just get in touch; we do really want to hear from you.

E-mail enquiries@developingpotential.co.uk or lessons@successfullives.co.uk

Or why not call us on 0044 (0) 20 3303 0496. We look forward to talking with you.

# CHAPTER ELEVEN: BECOME YOUR OWN PERFORMANCE COACH

## Coaching Rationale and Philosophy

What is coaching? The word 'coaching' means different things to different people, but the one consistent theme that runs throughout, is its aim to enhance performance.

Many people identify coaching with education, where a tutor encourages and gives instruction to help a student pass examinations, or with a sports coach who shares technical expertise and experience with their performers.

The modern coach, however, is more than just an instructor who gives the benefit of their knowledge and experience. The modern coach starts with the understanding that the person being coached is not just a passive learner, but has their own interests, capabilities, and ways of learning.

It is the coach's role to facilitate their learning and help improve their performance.

Outstanding coaches and teachers actually hold two agendas in their minds. Firstly, their own agenda to help the student learn through their expertise and knowledge and secondly, the student's agenda i.e. their aims, interests and values.

It is balancing and bringing these two agendas together, which creates the most effective learning environment. The coach or teacher promotes learning and co-operation by asking questions that engage students, which in turn enables them to think for themselves. This questioning raises their awareness of what they want, and what they need, and encourages them to choose to take responsibility for their actions.

## Rationale for Coaching

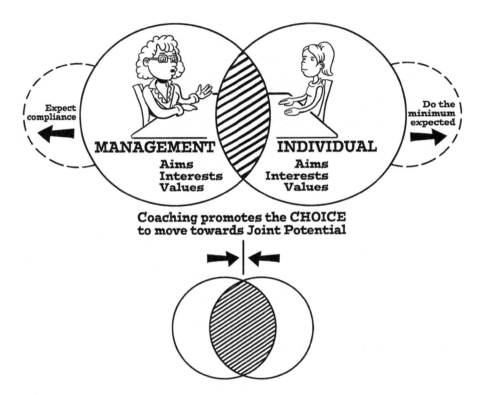

The purpose of coaching is to encourage improved performance from individuals, teams, and organisations (schools). One of the keys to success is to build relationships and positive attitudes, where people give freely of their time and energy to achieve common agreed goals. We sometimes refer to this as discretionary effort.

In the figure on page 168, Rationale for Coaching, we show two circles and each has the words aims, interests, and values within them. This is to demonstrate that individuals (staff/students) and management have their own agendas. Traditionally, management pushes their agenda and expects compliance. The downside with this approach is that it doesn't encourage individuals to contribute from choice.

As a result, as managers and teachers push for this compliance, focusing only on their own aims, interests and values, the people they lead or their students start to do the minimum expected.

So the aim of coaching is to bring the two parties (circles) together as you see in the bottom part of the diagram. It is through open and honest conversations, that each side shares their interests, and hopes and then works towards joint aims.

When managers and teachers also focus on the agenda of other individuals, it will result in an increase in what we call discretionary effort. That is students will give more of their own time and effort freely.

In schools it is important that leadership teams explain their agenda and also take note of teachers' and others' needs and

*When managers and teachers also focus on the agenda of other individuals, it will result in an increase in what we call discretionary effort.*

aspirations, creating a win/win scenario, where discretionary effort is given and both sides are aligned to an agreed vision.

## The Power of Coaching

The coaching journey begins with a basic philosophy (see the figure, Coaching Philosophy - the ice-cream cone). It is important for all coaches and leaders to start with a worldview, which is positive and is based on ethical values and a sense of serving others rather than just self-interest.

The next level encompasses beliefs, where everyone is deemed to have potential and that life is full of opportunities and abundance. Coaching behaviours such as asking, involving, and listening, come out of a positive worldview and beliefs. The outcomes from this way of being and doing are enhancing performance, learning, creativity, relationships and motivation.

In the past, unenlightened managers or teachers have tended to work on a philosophy, which is described on the left-hand side of the ice cream cone. In essence, it is self-centred around own interests, rather than being performer centred.

Often driven by fear or a feeling that others won't do what is needed, this approach leads to people waiting to be told what to do.

Its focus is on win/lose (as we discussed earlier), criticism and fear. This unfortunately leads to a blame culture, where people become compliant and dependent on their teacher, parents or friends.

As a result, performance and results suffer and are usually well below those that could be achieved.

## Coaching Philosophy

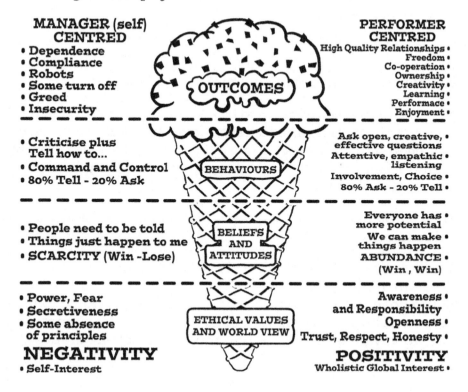

**MANAGER (self) CENTRED**
- Dependence
- Compliance
- Robots
- Some turn off
- Greed
- Insecurity

- Criticise plus Tell how to...
- Command and Control
- 80% Tell - 20% Ask

- People need to be told
- Things just happen to me
- SCARCITY (Win -Lose)

- Power, Fear
- Secretiveness
- Some absence of principles

**NEGATIVITY**
- Self-Interest

OUTCOMES

BEHAVIOURS

BELIEFS AND ATTITUDES

ETHICAL VALUES AND WORLD VIEW

**PERFORMER CENTRED**
- High Quality Relationships
- Freedom
- Co-operation
- Ownership
- Creativity
- Learning
- Performace
- Enjoyment

- Ask open, creative, effective questions
- Attentive, empathic listening
- Involvement, Choice
- 80% Ask - 20% Tell

- Everyone has more potential
- We can make things happen
- ABUNDANCE (Win , Win)

- Awareness and Responsibility
- Openness
- Trust, Respect, Honesty

**POSITIVITY**
- Wholistic Global Interest

But it doesn't have to be that way and people can be taught to coach themselves. Imagine the impact this will have on your students, if they are able to raise their own awareness of what they want and take responsibility for the results they want to achieve.

They can work towards achieving Olympian performance in whatever field they choose.

We share some exercises below that will help you build this skill in your students. These are a snapshot of ten lessons we have developed to teach coaching to young people, and that are available as part of our resilience and employability curriculum, called the Successful Lives programme (you can find out more at www.successfullives.co.uk).

## Exercise 1
Ask your students, in pairs, to discuss what they think Awareness and Responsibility mean.

An answer for **awareness** is to be conscious of and understand an issue or situation; and for **responsibility** it is after awareness has been gained, people choose to respond to a situation by taking action. In other words, people have the ability to respond or respond-ability.

Now explain to your students the aims and purpose of this exercise.

The purpose of coaching is to improve performance through helping to increase the awareness of the person being coached and therefore giving them the choice to take responsibility. You can only consciously change something you are aware of, so all change starts with self-awareness.

### Developing awareness
Ask your students to "freeze." Tell them. "Do not move and think about the following questions."

Ask, "How comfortable is your sitting position now?" (Body) Give a score 1 – 10 where one is very uncomfortable and ten very comfortable.

Further exploratory questions: Ask them, "Were you aware that you were comfortable/ uncomfortable? When did you become aware that you felt like this? Did you do anything about it?"

Now ask, "How are you feeling now?" (Emotion) Give a score 1 – 10 where one is very unhappy and ten very happy.

Further exploratory questions: Ask them, "Were you conscious of how you felt? If yes, how can this help you?"

Now ask, "What are you thinking about at the moment?" (Mind) Give a score 1 – 10 where one is thinking about something unrelated to this lesson and ten when you are focusing on the lesson.

Further exploratory questions: Ask them, "Why were you thinking about that? Was it important or relevant to you?"

Now ask, "How motivated are you feeling?" (Spirit) Give a score 1 – 10 where one is very unmotivated and ten very motivated.

Exploratory questions: Ask them, "What are you actually motivated about? Is it of high importance to you?"

Now ask your students to discuss in pairs or small groups, their thoughts and experiences of these questions and answers. What did it make them think about?

Once you are more aware of your situation, you can then make a choice of how you respond. For example, in order to change position, you can think about why you are feeling as you are and then do something about it. Alternatively, if you are thinking about something that isn't relevant, you can change your focus.

The key point is that successful people are highly aware, particularly of what they want to achieve, and choose to take personal responsibility for their life choices.

**Taking responsibility**
Ask students to discuss how they might change their position, how they are feeling, what they are thinking about and their current motivation once they become aware of it.

Ask them to feedback to you, regarding what this might mean for them in lessons. For example, if they are going to a lesson that they don't enjoy, how can they respond differently and more positively?

Ask your students to take an example from three areas of their life – school, home, and friends.

Then ask them to reflect on a current situation from each area that they are currently aware of and how they could take responsibility for making changes.

Once completed, students can share their views in pairs and then as a class.

Then discuss as a group when it is useful to be told what to do and when it might be better to be asked, so you can work it out for yourself.

## The Coaching Dance

This is where a teacher or coach can help improve performance by either telling or asking.

The coaching dance was developed by Dr David Hemery CBE, Olympic Gold Medallist and co-founder of our business, Developing Potential.

Generally, when parents, teachers, coaches and later in their life managers, try to support people, they tend to work on their own agenda and be very directive (Tell), which is on the left-hand side of the diagram on page 175.

For example moving through the first four areas of the coaching dance above (Motivate, Goals/Targets, Feedback and Learning), you can ask your students the following questions and use any of the examples, e.g. parent, teacher, coach, manager.

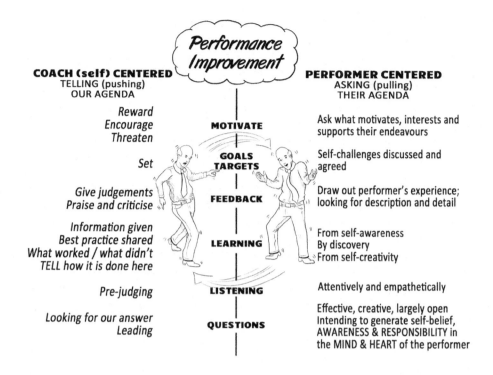

**COACH (self) CENTERED**
TELLING (pushing)
OUR AGENDA

**PERFORMER CENTERED**
ASKING (pulling)
THEIR AGENDA

Reward
Encourage
Threaten

**MOTIVATE**

Ask what motivates, interests and supports their endeavours

Set

**GOALS
TARGETS**

Self-challenges discussed and agreed

Give judgements
Praise and criticise

**FEEDBACK**

Draw out performer's experience; looking for description and detail

Information given
Best practice shared
What worked / what didn't
TELL how it is done here

**LEARNING**

From self-awareness
By discovery
From self-creativity

Pre-judging

**LISTENING**

Attentively and empathetically

Looking for our answer
Leading

**QUESTIONS**

Effective, creative, largely open
Intending to generate self-belief,
AWARENESS & RESPONSIBILITY in
the MIND & HEART of the performer

Under the *motivate* heading ask, "What does a parent, teacher, coach or manager usually do to help motivate you?"

Answers may include: reward, encourage, praise or they may negatively threaten.

Under the *goals/targets* heading ask, "What does a parent, teacher, coach or manager do in the area of goals and targets?"

The answer is they normally set them.

Ask them, "How many of you set yourselves goals?"

Under the *feedback* heading ask, "What does a parent, teacher, coach or manager do to give feedback?"

Answers may include: criticise, give judgments and provide information and suggestions.

Under the *learning heading* ask, "Generally what does a parent, teacher, coach or manager do to help learning?"

Answers may include: instruct, share best practice and demonstrate. All the answers shared above, can be placed on the tell or left-hand side of the coaching dance.

This left-hand side is the parent, teacher, coach, manager side, which usually focuses on their agenda and is about push and telling. Most parents, teachers, coaches and managers largely limit themselves to this side.

For example, when we are young, our parents tell us what to do, then our teachers tell us and finally our managers tell us. As a result, the learned behaviour is to tell, not ask.

Ask your students how often they are asked what they want to do when it comes to school, deciding rules and many other important things?

The right-hand side is about the students' agenda and is about pulling from them and asking.

So the teacher would ASK open questions rather than tell, for example; What goals would you like to achieve? What motivates you? What feedback would be helpful for you and what would you like to learn?

The skills that coaches and successful leaders use for effective communication are questioning and listening, (which are also shown on the coaching dance diagram). The information below is for you and depending on the age of students; you can also ask them the questions.

Question: "What types of questions do we use on the tell side?"

Answer: Often closed (yes or no answers) or leading questions, e.g. would you agree with me that this is the best option for you?

Question: "What types of questions do we use on the ask (right-hand) side?"

Answer: Mostly open questions, e.g. what, where, when, etc. These questions are intended to generate *Awareness* and *Responsibility* in the mind of the performer.

Question: "When a parent, teacher, coach or manager is on the tell side, how does he/she listen?"

Answer: Usually for their right answer (not necessarily the student's answer).

Question: "How would you listen on the ask side?"

Answer: Really listening empathically and with 100% attention.

Question: "How does a parent, teacher, coach, manager help the student learn on the ask side?"

Answer: Ask them how and what they might want to learn, to help them self-discover, and to be creative.

Question: "What does a parent, teacher, coach, manager do to motivate on the ask side?

Answer: Simply ask what motivates them?

Question: "What does a parent, teacher, coach, manager do to set goals and targets on the ask side?"

Answer: Ask the performer what they want to achieve and discuss and agree the goals.

Question: "What does a parent, teacher, coach, manager do to give feedback on the ask side?"

Answer: Ask the student how they think it went first. Draw from their experience and look for their description and detail (before sharing information or your own view).

There is NO right or wrong side on which to be. However, the right-hand side has been generally neglected. The best way forward is to dance between both sides as appropriate and with the emphasis of always starting and finishing on the ask side, to help students to think for themselves first and then take personal responsibility for their learning and actions.

Sometimes, people say that it takes too much time to ask and you might want to think about the long-term as well as the short-term.

For example under the heading *help you learn*, someone giving (telling) you an answer might be quicker, but in the long-term if you only give answers, students become reliant on you the teacher and don't learn for themselves. This will take more time over the long-term.

How can you help your students to learn to ask themselves good questions so they can be their own coach, think for themselves, help solve their own problems and achieve their goals?

### Questioning
There are two different types of ways to ask questions, if we exclude leading questions that encourage people to

give you the answer you want. These are called open and closed questions.

On page 180 are two columns of words – the left-hand column (1) are words that start open questions and the right-hand column (2) words that start closed questions.

You can ask the following questions and students can use thumbs up, their hands or coloured cards to indicate if they feel that, the question is open, or closed.

1) Will (2) you be going out at the weekend? (Yes/no = closed).

2) What (1) is (2) your goal for today? (Open).

3) Are (2) you going out with friends? (Yes/no = closed).

4) Is (2) it going to rain? (Yes/no = closed).

5) How (1) will (2) you move forward on your issue? (Open).

6. Who (1) can (2) support you? (Open).

> *There are two different types of ways to ask questions, if we exclude leading questions that encourage people to give you the answer you want. These are called open and closed questions.*

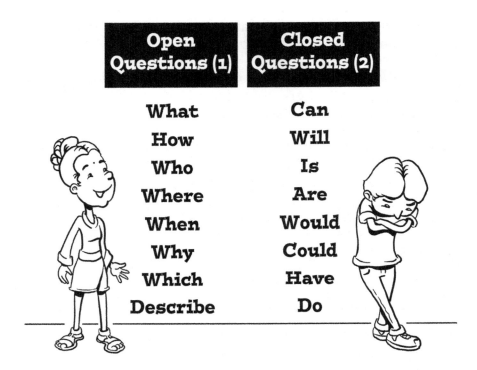

| Open Questions (1) | Closed Questions (2) |
|---|---|
| What | Can |
| How | Will |
| Who | Is |
| Where | Are |
| When | Would |
| Why | Could |
| Which | Have |
| Describe | Do |

Using words from column 1 followed by words from column 2, often creates an effective question.

Now ask your students to compose five questions that they would ask if they had an opportunity to interview their hero. First, they will need to write down the name of their hero, and then the five questions they would like to ask them.

Once they have a list of five questions, ask them to discuss them with a partner and to consider if the questions they have written down will allow them to gain the most information from their hero.

Then ask them to compare the questions they have asked with the open and closed question list of starting words above. Did their questions mostly begin with words from column 1 (open) or column 2 (closed)?

Ask them how many started with words from column 1 and also included words from column 2.

It is best to start with open questions, as this opens a conversation and will support them in finding lots of information from their hero. Once they have broad themes, then closed questions can help to narrow down to specific points.

In addition you can use the G.R.O.W model as a framework to ask effective questions (see the GROW questions in chapter 7), particularly when you want to create a plan.

**Listening**
Ask students to work in groups of three – one listener, one speaker, and one observer.

Ask the groups to discuss and answer the following question, "Why is being able to listen well an important skill for successful people?"

Answers might include, learning more, understanding other people and their points of view, finding better ideas and solutions, building rapport, influencing other people, greater enjoyment and others more willing to help and support you.

Each of them will have the opportunity to speak, listen and observe and ask each of them to choose a topic that they will be able to talk about. Examples might include, a favourite sport, a hobby, a holiday, what they did at the weekend, a favourite book, television programme or film, or something of your (or their) choice.

Ask the observer to look at what is happening and how each of them changes their body language during the conversation.

Ask each person to talk for one or two minutes and once this has been completed and all students have had a turn, ask the following two questions. You can discuss in groups and/or share as a class.

"When you were speaking how did the person listening make you feel?"

"What, if anything, would you have liked them to have done differently?"

This exercise will help raise their awareness of what it takes to be an effective listener and show that this is a skill that can be learned.

Follow up by asking, "What gets in the way of effective listening?"

Answers may include distractions, their own self talk, lack of interest in the speaker or what they are talking about, they have something more important on their mind, and they are too busy.

Then ask, "What are some things they can do to be more effective at listening?"

Answers may include, focus on the speaker, focus on the subject, control their self talk, practise, be genuinely interested in what others have to say, make time (so if no time now, agree another time rather than listening while playing on a phone or tablet) and really concentrate.

Like some of the areas we covered in building resilience, it is about creating effective and positive habits.

There is much more to effective coaching and if you want an opportunity to access ten, one- hour lessons to use with your students, then please visit www.successfullives.co.uk. These are part of our resilience and employability curriculum and are based on our work with elite performers for over twenty years. These include CEOs, senior leaders in business, school leaders and Olympic athletes and teams.

We have provided the basics within this chapter for you to help your students to start to coach themselves and their peers. This is one of the best skills you can give them and will also build their resilience.  It will allow them to continuously ask questions of themselves, listen to their own thoughts, give themselves feedback, set goals, plan and take action.

By developing this as a positive daily habit, they will do more of their own thinking and find more of their own solutions, in other words become self-directed learners.

# APPENDIX: THE SEVEN STEPS – A QUICK REFERENCE GUIDE

This is a quick reference guide covering all seven steps. If you wish to remind yourself about the more specific details within the steps, you can refer to the chapters for information.

<u>**Two steps you can take immediately:**</u>
Every teacher can do two things immediately to help their students build resilience that leads toward greater success. They can:

1. Work towards developing a positive mindset.

2. Develop a positive learning culture in the classroom.

## Step 1 Place
We often keep ourselves in a place of comfort and security, yet to develop our potential, we need to take risks and step outside our comfort zone. To support this we can:

- Share experiences of when you and your students stepped out of your/their comfort zones. What was the outcome and the learning to be used next time something new is attempted?

- Ask the students questions around what they might like to do?

- If they are nervous about trying something new, ask them what they could do, to take a first step.

To take your experience a step further, you can give students the task of thinking about something they would like to do and determine:

- Why it excites them?
- What might their journey look like?
- What obstacles might they face and how will they overcome them?
- What is their plan and first action?
- Who might be a supporter and help them?
- What might success look and feel like for them?
- What lessons might they learn and how will they apply these in their future?

These elements can help create an opportunity for stepping outside their comfort zone for every student. You can also consider factors such as:

- How do you make sure that the risks you take are appropriate, when stepping out of your comfort zone?
- Why is change and trying new experiences exciting?
- How can change help you learn about yourself and others?
- What is one thing you might like to do more of or differently today?

Perhaps you can end the discussion with students giving one action they will take today. You could act as a role model for them, showing them your own examples of how you tried new things. It would also be helpful to follow up on their progress to see how they do and to continue to support them.

### Win/Lose Vs. Win/Learn

Most people operate on a win/lose basis. You see it in sport, business and within your everyday lives. You try something and win or lose, succeed or fail. The press or media don't help, often showing people to be heroes or villains. There seems to be little middle ground.

There is often a lot of negative emotion and publicity (even if it is just in front of friends) associated with trying something new, with the possibility of being seen as a failure or loser.

It is more helpful to focus on developing a win/learn mindset. When you try something new, you will know what result you want but you don't always achieve it on the first attempt. It may be a better or worse result than you would have liked and the important lesson is, to adopt an attitude, which says you might have (failed) this time, but what did you learn and how can you use this in trying again. The important questions to ask yourself are, "What did I learn from the experience and what would I do differently next time?"

Creating a positive win/learn mindset removes negative emotion and the fear of failure. It does take practise to make this an everyday habit, but once you change your thinking, you will wonder why you ever found it so difficult to try new things.


## Step 2 Passion

Every child is curious and has an innate desire to learn. If given the opportunity they will develop interests and it is their passion that drives progress and achievement.

Showing young people how to identify their passions and how to go about pursuing them, is a real gift that a teacher can offer. This is achieved through:

## Creating awareness

- Make a list of what they enjoy doing most and why.

- Take a moment to reflect on how some activities make them feel.

- Explore ideas of how they can add more or different activities into their life.

## Building confidence

Confidence is what allows us to pursue our passions, even when we fear failure or setbacks. Sometimes we need to tell ourselves we can do something and just have a go!

One of the key roles of a teacher or parent is to show that you believe in them first before they begin to believe in themselves.

While strategic thinking comes from your head, passion comes from the heart. The heart is also the place where values are held and they determine behaviour. There are three intrinsic values (motivators) that support passion and they are enjoyment, learning and performance.

## Enjoyment

Some students become disengaged from their schoolwork or life in general, because they don't find any relevance or interest in what they are doing. Therefore, it's really important to help them find things they are interested in and passionate about and the more students can see that school subjects will help them in the future, the more they will see their relevancy. It does take effort and young people need to explore lots of different activities to find what they enjoy.

There is also a caveat that sometimes we have to do things in life that don't include our real interests, so part of being successful, is to find at least some elements that will engage them.

## Learning
Every child is born with natural curiosity, for example most two-year-old children ask 'WHY' questions repeatedly, to find out about the world in which they live. Yet formal education for some seems to dampen their enthusiasm for learning, because they are told what to do and are only rewarded by the right answers. Resilience is developed by learning through trial and error, by making mistakes and finding multiple answers to questions. Can you as a teacher reignite their passion for learning, by asking and involving them more in the discovery of knowledge?

## Performance
Every child likes to perform, develop skills and be successful. If we look at Maslow's hierarchy of needs, having self-esteem is high on the agenda of psychological wellness. There is a saying that success breeds success and if a young person can find a passion and interest and develop it, they can use that experience to learn and perform in other areas of life.

It is also helpful for young people to appreciate that what is a passion for them, might not be something which everyone enjoys or in which they have an interest. To understand other people's passion, it is also good to develop the value of empathy.

## Empathy
Empathy is the ability to be able to place yourself in another's situation and understand what they are feeling and experiencing. Three ways to help students gain empathy:

- Imagine being in someone else's shoes and seeing things from their point of view.

- Focus on being open-minded not judgemental.
- Share with them the power of listening to others.

## Step 3 Purpose

While achievement is at the heart of fulfilling potential, having a real sense of meaning and purpose gives us the power and reason to pursue our goals.

Start a conversation with students, so they can understand their purpose. Ask your students what having a purpose in life means. You might like to use the following statements as part of your discussion.

- Purpose sometimes involves being part of a cause that's bigger than you.
- Purpose is about using your talents in the service of others.
- Purpose is focused around doing things that are important and meaningful to you.

In small groups ask students to discuss the following:

- What might give them a sense of meaning and purpose?
- What service might they like to offer to others?
- What is really important to them?

Discuss examples of people who demonstrate living their purpose. Focus on qualities such as:

- How they recognise their purpose.
- Their motivation.

- Their dedication.

- Their determination to pursue their purpose.

- Their persistence in overcoming obstacles.

- Their achievements.

Next, you might want to focus on what purpose means to individual students. Create a list of items that each student can discuss (this follows from the earlier discussion when similar questions were asked as a group). Ask them individually:

- What is their purpose?

- What might give them a sense of meaning in their life?

- How might they be of service to others?

If students need more time to find their purpose, here are some thoughts to help:

- Who could be role models for them?

- What do they need to do to explore and find their purpose?

- What areas of personal interest might help them find their purpose?

In the third and final session of purpose, you might ask students to create a story or visualisation, which would incorporate living their purpose. They can use their senses including their sixth sense of intuition.

- Sight – What do they see themselves doing?

- Touch – How do they feel about achieving their purpose?

- Sound – What positive things do they hear people saying about them?
- Intuition – What does their intuition (their gut feeling) tell them about their purpose?

## Step 4 People

Life will always be full of challenges. We can be successful on our own, but the help of caring people who understand our dreams and goals can make a big difference.

Teachers can discuss the importance of people and how they can:

- Help them find their passion and purpose.
- Influence or persuade them positively or negatively.
- Be a source of inspiration.
- Be supportive in difficult times.

Ask your students, "Why might it be important to have a support team?"

Some common answers are likely to be:

- Support teams give advice and help.
- Support teams help overcome difficulties.
- Support teams ask great questions that make them think for themselves.
- Support teams are good listeners.
- Support teams can help teach skills and share knowledge your students don't yet have.
- Support teams can help make good decisions.

Next, you might include specific examples of support teams, from personal experiences, school, businesses, sport and any areas of life. For example, an Olympic athlete has a coach, doctor, psychologist, physiotherapist, masseuse or masseur, administration support, team officials and probably an agent or manager. Ask students to think about:

- Some people that are truly supporting them. (*Not everyone is easy to identify*).

- How those people help them?

- What support they might need in the future?

- Who else might help them?

In order to decide whom you want in your support team, it would be good to define the characteristics that would make people a great supporter. This might include:

Authenticity, balance, commitment, compassion, concern for others, courage, creativity, empathy, excellence, fairness, freedom, friendship, generosity, genuineness, happiness, health, honesty, humour, integrity, kindness, knowledge, loyalty, openness, perseverance, respect for others, responsibility, service to others, and trust.

An exercise you can do to help your students think about their values and the values they want in a supporter is:

- Ask each student to choose three values that are important to them.

- Share these and pick the top three values in the class. You can do this by putting up a list and asking students to vote for their top three.

- Come up with examples of how students can demonstrate they are living to these values through their behaviours. What will be seen every day by others?

From there, ask students. How they feel when someone behaves in a way that contradicts their values? How do they deal with people who don't have the same values as them?

The last part of the activity focuses on the differences and similarities between people. Ask your students what ways they think people are different or similar, based on the following areas:

- Interests.
- Behaviour.
- Values and beliefs.
- Whether they are outgoing or shy.
- Their desire to lead or only participate.
- Respecting rules or preferring to be rule breakers.
- Being methodical or just getting things completed quickly.

The way people behave and act, affects relationships. Talk with the class about how they can build relationships. Focus on points such as:

- Understanding others.
- Showing tolerance.
- Having empathy.
- Being patience.
- Developing a positive mindset.

Your students will now have a strong grasp of the fundamentals of a support team and how they can also be a helpful contributor to the support team of others.

## Step 5 Planning
Having a vision and purpose is powerful, but without concrete goals and an action plan, they are but a dream.

### 1. Determine why planning is important
Ask your students:

- Why they think that planning is important?
- To share when they have planned or not planned for an event and what the results were.
- What needs to be in a plan to make it successful?
- If circumstances change what do they need to do with their plan?

### 2. Make time to G.R.O.W.
Demonstrate and help students understand the G.R.O.W. model by walking them through it.

As an exercise, you can ask them to think about something that they want to achieve and use the answers to the questions, to make a plan.

### G is for GOAL:
This is where you'll determine what you really want to achieve, focusing on:

- What do you really want to achieve?
- When do you want to achieve it by?
- What will success look like?

- How much control do you have over achieving this goal?
- What might be some milestones along the way?
- How motivating is this goal for you? It needs to be something you really want if you are going to stick at it.

## R is for REALITY:
Evaluate your present situation:

- In relation to your goal what is happening now?
- Who else might be involved in you achieving your goal?
- What have you done already, including:
  o Action you have taken so far
  o Research you have carried out
  o Thoughts that are yet to be put into action.
- What were the results of your past action?

## O is for OPTION:
Options are merely ideas and thoughts on how to achieve your goals.

- What can you do? Have your students take some time to list at least five ideas that will help them achieve their goal.
- Once they have written down a number of ideas, ask them to rate each one on a scale of 1 – 10, with ten being the one they are most enthusiastic about and one being the least desirable (in their opinion).

*The highest ranking options are the ones that the students should focus on pursuing first. Explain that all the other options may also be good, but they are more likely to complete the ones where they have the most interest.*

**W is for WILL:**

Help your students find ways to keep their plan's momentum moving forward in a positive direction. Consider the following questions:

- What will you do now to move towards your goal?
- What is your first action step?
- When will you take that step?
- What support might you need?
- What obstacles might you need to overcome?
- How committed are you to taking your fist step?

*And now that you've made the commitment, it's time to rate on a scale of 1 – 10 how committed you are to take the action steps necessary. Ten is fully committed and one shows no commitment.*

*If you don't score a 10, then there is some sort of blockage and you are unlikely to achieve the first step or goal. You will need to think again, about what you need to do to make this more motivating and a 10 before you proceed. You can then put down further steps and build your full plan or just take it step by step.*

## Step 6 Positive Mindset

Mindset is important. It can be our greatest asset or what holds us back. Teaching young people to believe in their abilities, to have confidence, and address life with a positive approach, is the foundation of resilience and success.

A way to start a conversation is to share this saying by Henry Ford:

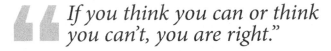 *If you think you can or think you can't, you are right."*

Discuss how people often create a self-fulfilling prophecy through what they tell themselves. When students know that what they think or say out loud may often come true, it may encourage them to keep their thoughts more positive than negative.

Start with small group activities and ensure that:

- Everyone can think about what the saying means to them.
- Everyone has a chance to respond and discuss.

Perhaps you as the teacher can share:

- When you had an experience where you thought you couldn't do something and found out you were right.
- When you had an experience where you thought you could do something that was a bit frightening and you were right.

Now ask them to share a time when they had a personal experience based on the saying above and how it made them feel.

Some examples you may find shared by your students might include:

- Playing a solo in a band.
- Trying out for a sport.
- Auditioning for a play.
- Riding that big rollercoaster.

- Not talking to someone because you were too shy.

- Not asking a question because you were afraid.

Take two or three of the scenarios and ask your students to think about how they might overcome a situation where they felt that they could not do or try something:

- What is the worst thing that could have happened?

- What could you have done differently?

- Were other people encouraging you to try or not?

- Would you do it today if you had the chance?

**Win/Learn versus Win/Lose**
We covered this earlier and we want to reinforce it here. This concept can be shared in the classroom and as a result, everyone will gain a better understanding of what it means.

In society, we are often faced with heroes or villains, or successful people or failures. Yet in order to be successful, we have to try new things and often fail at the first attempt. If we don't get the result we had hoped for, we must not beat ourselves up, but take the learning and move on. Success normally comes by making mistakes and persisting in our efforts to make progress. It is important to remember that we are defined by who we are as a human being and not by what we do or achieve in life.

We need to develop learners and not losers. Decide on a scenario to share with your students. Here are a few ideas for you:

- Suzie tries out for the basketball or soccer team, but does not make it.

- Dan gets a lower grade on his test than he would have liked.

- Jennifer was made fun of by some girls she was trying to make friends with.

- Sam played some poor notes in his first saxophone lesson and wants to give up.

Explore what happens in the scenarios using the win/lose mentality. Discuss:

- What thoughts do you experience when you do not succeed?

- How do you feel emotionally?

- Do you accept that you lost and never try that again or something else?

Discuss how you can take a scenario and make it a win/learn situation. Discuss ideas such as:

- What you do when you don't achieve what you want?

- How do you feel when you achieve something that was difficult to do?

- What is the difference between a win/learn and win/lose attitude?

- What has been a recent example where you have turned a win/lose into a win/learn situation?

### Positive self talk

Every person has a voice in their heads (self talk) that helps them choose what to do or not to do. The challenge is to make this voice more positive than negative.

An example you could give of a negative voice in someone's head might be:

> *I'd really love to take art class, but I'm no good. I shouldn't do it. I don't want to embarrass myself."*

Follow that up with a positive example of how a student could learn to communicate with the voice in their head.

> *I'd really love to take art class. I choose to have that experience and improve my skills."*

There is a significant difference between these two voices and people often gravitate towards the negative. The words we use are an important influence on whether we achieve our goals. Ask your students to give you some phrases or words that they would see as negative.

Here are some examples to share with your students:

- I can't.
- I shouldn't.
- I'm not good enough.
- I don't have the energy.
- I'm hopeless or the situation is hopeless.
- They would never let me.
- I'm useless and no good at anything.

Ask them to share some positive statements and ask them to explain why they are better choices. Here are a few examples:

- I can choose to.
- I will.
- It is possible.

- That interests me.
- I choose to experience that.
- I expect to have fun and enjoy myself.
- I like trying new things.

You can have a great discussion about how much better positive self talk makes you feel and the powerful effect it has on performance.

Ask students to consider:

- What are they saying in their self talk? Is it positive or negative?
- What can they do to make sure that positive thoughts are present more often than negative ones and eventually most of the time?
- Keeping a diary or writing a note about the good things they do or say to themselves.
- Writing down three things they have done well at the end of each day.

## Strengths

Helping students develop an awareness of their strengths will also have a positive impact on their self-esteem, resilience and attitude. The following exercises will help pinpoint them:

## What are your strengths?

- What do you enjoy doing?
- What can you do if only a little?
- What are you naturally good at?

- What do other people say that you are good at?

- In what areas do you have a real interest?

**How can you use your strengths to maintain a positive mindset and to achieve the things that you want?**
In life you tend to succeed at things that you enjoy most or find easier to do.  It's a good way to build your self-confidence and self-esteem.   If you can identify your strengths and develop these areas, you can use the learning to develop other activities in your life.

**What are you going to do differently as a result of this exercise?**
This is where students can take action and responsibility for doing something that is positive for themselves and geared towards their success.  Remember the first sign of insanity, is to do the same things and expect a different result (a saying accredited by some to Einstein).

So ask your students, "What can they do to build their own positive mindset?"

An example: develop persistence.

William Edward Hickson is a British educator who is credited with popularising the proverb: *If at first you don't succeed, try, try, and try again.*  Persistence is about never giving up and it is necessary to apply this every day to achieve your goals and dreams.


## Step 7 Physical Action
Physical action has two dimensions; building physical capability and physically taking action to make things happen.

Let's look at building physical capability first and how it affects resilience. Ask this question:

Imagine you are tired, hungry, and thirsty. How are you feeling and how might it affect you and your performance?

Some typical responses might be:

- If I'm hungry I can't concentrate very well, especially in class.
- When I'm tired I can get into a bad mood.
- If I'm tired I just want to sit down and do nothing or watch television.
- Sometimes when I'm thirsty and dehydrated I get a headache.

You can share some positive solutions that maintain physical wellness and energy. Ask the following question to start the discussion. Are you more likely to be less or more resilient during these times?

Students will know that they are less resilient when they are tired or hungry. This is where you can ask them for some 'fuel-up ideas', which might include:

- Getting enough sleep.
- Eating well and not having too many fats or sugars in their diet.
- Making sure that they eat breakfast every day.
- Drinking enough water throughout the day.
- Exercising daily (in some way).
- Walking more.

- Teaching them the 80/20 rule: it's okay to have treats at times, but keep a good balance, making them the exception rather than the norm.

Ask your students to write down the things that they currently do well in their daily lives and what they might do differently to enhance their energy.

The second part of step 7, physical action is **making things happen**.

Many students and adults have dreams and aspirations, but those who succeed in life take action. There is a saying that imperfect action beats perfect inaction every time.

While you may start with passion, motivation and a goal, it needs to be turned into results by using your willpower. However, the latest research[8] shows that people have only a limited amount of willpower and the way to overcome this is to create positive habits. It is these habits that enable you to do things almost unconsciously and mean you don't have to have an internal fight saying, 'will I or won't I do something'.

Setting habits and rules, also helps overcome obstacles. For example if you want to give up drinking coffee in order to be more healthy, you can just say to yourself my new rule is that I am not a coffee drinker and I don't drink coffee.

All change starts with self-awareness and asking ourselves questions and self-coaching is a great way to start the process. Using the GROW model will really help your students identify their goals, generate ideas and take action.

---

8  See the list of references on page 211 for details of the research suggesting willpower is a limited resource.

*Our last exercise is to choose a new habit through self-coaching.*

Students can choose to create a new positive habit. There are four steps required to form a new habit, which are:

1. *What is your reason to create a new habit?*
2. *What values support this change?*
3. *What is your plan to create the change?*
4. *What action steps do you need to take?*

For example if you want to become fitter.

1. Your reason may be to become more energised and enjoy life and achieve more.
2. Your supporting value could be to want a healthy lifestyle.
3. Your plan is to join a keep fit group.
4. Your action is to sign up today.

Once your students have created a new habit, you can help them make it more tangible in their minds. Ask them to either:

- Take a few minutes to imagine themselves acting out this new habit, feeling positive about themselves and achieving what they set out to do.

Or:

- Take some time to create a short story and write about their new habit and how it helps them succeed.

Teachers play an important role as you are the guardians of our young people and enable them to become successful.

We believe in a growth mindset, that all young people have enormous potential and that intelligence, both intellectual and emotional, is flexible and can be grown.

As we have already stated, past performance is no indicator of future success and we know from our experience that resilience and the habits of successful people can be taught.

We hope that this book has been of assistance and please do get in touch with any questions, feedback and success stories. We wish you and your students every future success.

**Les Duggan**                                        **Mark Solomons**

www.developingpotential.co.uk               www.successfullives.co.uk
E: enquiries@developingpotential.co.uk     E: lessons@successfullives.co.uk
Call 0044 (0) 20 3303 0496

# REFERENCE LIST

This research underpins some of the points made in the book and is referenced by footnotes at the bottom of the relevant pages.

Footnotes 1. & 3. Dr Barbara Fredrickson and her Positivity Ratio.

(i) Positivity by Barbara L. Fredrickson PH.D. Groundbreaking Research Reveals How to Embrace the Hidden Strength of Positive Emotions, Overcome Negativity, and Thrive. ISBN 1851687904

(ii) Fredrickson, B. L. (2013, July 15). Updated Thinking on Positivity Ratios. American Psychologist. Advance online publication. doi: 10.1037/a0033584

Footnotes 2. & 7. Single Focus of Champions – the following research is among many studies that highlight how multitasking reduces efficiency and performance.

(i) Charron S, Koechlin E. Divided representation of concurrent goals in the human frontal lobes. Science. 328(360), 360-363 (2010).

(ii) Rubinstein, J. S., Meyer, D. E. & Evans, J. E. (2001). Executive Control of Cognitive Processes in Task Switching. Journal of Experimental Psychology: Human Perception and Performance, 27, 763-797.

(iii) Rogers, R. & Monsell, S. (1995). The costs of a predictable switch between simple cognitive tasks. Journal of Experimental Psychology: General, 124, 207-231.

Footnote 4. The following research suggests eating three main meals a day may be the best option for most people.

(i) Effect of meal frequency on glucose and insulin excursions over the course of a day. Michael E. Holmstrup, Christopher M. Owens, Timothy J. Fairchild, Jill A. Kanaley. This reported that people eating fewer, larger meals, on average have lower blood/glucose levels.

(ii) Meal Frequency and Risk of Colorectal Cancer. Silvia Franceschi, Carlo La Vecchia, Ettore Bidoli, Eva Negri, and Renato Talamini. This reported a higher risk of colon cancer with more frequent eating.

(iii) The effect of breakfast type on total daily energy intake and body mass index: results from the Third National Health and Nutrition Examination Survey (NHANES III). Cho S, Dietrich M, Brown CJ, Clark CA, Block G. This reported a higher risk of obesity for those who skip breakfast.

(iv) Meal frequency and energy balance. Bellisle F, McDevitt R, Prentice A. M. This reported no decrease in energy from eating three main meals.

(v) International Society of Sports Nutrition position stand: meal frequency. Paul M La Bounty, Bill I Campbell, Jacob Wilson, Elfego Galvan, John Berardi, Susan M Kleiner, Richard B Kreider, Jeffrey R Stout, Tim Ziegenfuss, Marie Spano, Abbie Smith and Jose Antonio. This reported that spreading calories out over more than three meals doesn't appear to change body composition favourably. Eating breakfast, lunch and dinner each day may be optimal for controlling appetite and managing food intake.

Footnote 5. 'Spark!' How exercise will improve the performance of your brain. Dr John J. Ratey and Eric Hagerman. ISBN 1849161577

Footnotes 6. & 8. The following research is among that, which suggests that willpower is a limited resource.

(i) Ego depletion: Is the active self a limited resource? Baumeister, R., Bratslavsky, E., Muraven, M., and Tice, D.M. (1998). Journal of Personality and Social Psychology, 74(5), 1252-1265.

(ii) The strength model of self-control. Baumeister, Roy F.; Vohs, Kathleen D.; Tice, Dianne M. Current Directions in Psychological Science, Vol 16(6), Dec 2007, 351-355.

(iii) Effects of self-regulatory strength depletion on muscular performance and EMG activation. Bray, S.R., Ginis, K.A.M., Hicks, A.L., and Woodgate, J. (2008). Psychophysiology, 45, 337-343.

# ABOUT THE AUTHORS

Les Duggan and Mark Solomons both spent around 25 years working in the corporate world and ended their time as senior leaders, Les in Chocolate (Cadbury) and Mark in retail banking (Sainsbury's Bank).

They developed a passion for supporting others and helping them develop the attitudes, behaviours and skills for success. They have both spent many years leading others and subsequently working with successful leaders in business and education, as well as elite Olympian performers.

They noticed that successful people had a common set of traits and having spent many years helping 'older' people change the habits of a lifetime, to achieve the things they wanted, they realised that it would be more effective to share these skills with young people so they could use them for their lifetime.

They have developed a set of lessons for schools that form a resilience and employability curriculum and through doing this work, wanted to capture some of their key learning, which they have done through writing and publishing this book.

Les is married to Joanna and has three grown-up children, Amanda, Rhiannon and Joss, as well as two grandchildren Rowen and Fenn.

Mark is married to Amanda and has two teenagers, Matthew and Rebecca, and a dog (Bella).

CPSIA information can be obtained at www.ICGtesting.com
Printed in the USA
LVOW04s1512260315

432156LV00018B/718/P